THE EXCAVATIONS
AT QUMRAN

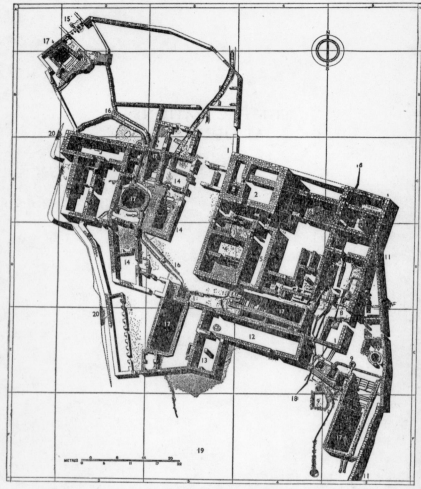

PLAN OF THE BUILDINGS AT KHIRBET QUMRAN AT THE TIME OF THE EARTHQUAKE (*From 'Revue Biblique', October 1956*)

1-1. Corners of walls of earlier Iron Age settlement (eighth–sixth century B.C.)
2. Tower.
3. Stairway to upper floor.
4. Hall with low bench along walls.
5. Scriptorium (scribes' room).
6. Kitchen.
7. Dye-works.
8. Laundry.
9-9. Pottery workshops.
10. Pottery ovens.

11. Boundary wall between buildings and cemetery.
12. Assembly hall.
13. Store-room for crockery.
14-14. Workshops.
15. Entry of aqueduct.
16-16. Main conduit.
17-17. Large cisterns.
18-18. Trace of earthquake-fault.
19. Southern terrace.
20-20. Retaining wall along western ravine.

J. VAN DER PLOEG, O.P.

THE EXCAVATIONS
AT QUMRAN

*A Survey of the Judaean
Brotherhood and its Ideas*

Translated by Kevin Smyth, S.J.

LONGMANS, GREEN AND CO
LONDON · NEW YORK · TORONTO

LONGMANS, GREEN AND CO LTD
6 & 7 CLIFFORD STREET LONDON W 1
THIBAULT HOUSE THIBAULT SQUARE CAPE TOWN
605–611 LONSDALE STREET MELBOURNE C 1

LONGMANS, GREEN AND CO INC
55 FIFTH AVENUE NEW YORK 3

LONGMANS, GREEN AND CO
20 CRANFIELD ROAD TORONTO 16

ORIENT LONGMANS PRIVATE LTD
CALCUTTA BOMBAY MADRAS
DELHI HYDERABAD DACCA

First published by Het Spectrum, Utrecht 1957 under
the title " Vondsten in de Woestijn van Juda."

This edition first published 1958

PRINTED IN GREAT BRITAIN BY JARROLD AND SONS
LTD. NORWICH. NIHIL OBSTAT: HUBERTUS RICHARDS,
S.T.L., L.S.S., CENSOR DEPUTATUS. IMPRIMATUR:
E. MORROGH BERNARD, VIC. GEN., WESTMONASTERII,
DIE 18A DECEMBRIS, 1957.

To the memory of my mother
Petronella Anna van der Ploeg-Snijers
19.1.1880–11.1.1957

CONTENTS

LIST OF PLATES

Frontispiece

Plan of the ruins of Khirbet Qumran.

between pp. 76 and 77

between pp. 140 and 141

PREFACE

There is still no book in the Western world which can arouse such interest and even excitement as the Bible. For Christians it remains the Book beyond compare, and even those who no longer count themselves Christian still hold it in high regard. The Western world may have become de-Christianized to a great extent, especially in externals, but it still has some memories of its origins, into which Christianity is so closely woven that the West still feels its influence.

When therefore in 1947 a number of ancient biblical manuscripts were found in the desert of Judah, not far from the Dead Sea, and when it soon appeared that this was only the beginning of 'the greatest manuscript discovery of modern times', public interest was immediately awakened, and showed itself in the quick reaction of Press, radio and television. The fact that the Bible was involved appealed to the faith—or the imagination—of millions. The origins of Christianity, it was claimed, were to be seen in a new light, and it seemed to those who had little esteem for Christianity that they were offered a chance for which they had been long waiting. Not only the trained scholars but the many publicists who are eager to popularize the results of research came into action. These were soon joined by the even larger groups for whom the subject, Christianity and the Bible, was of immediate significance.

The result was that not ten years have passed since the first discoveries, and already a literature has sprung up on the subject and its corollaries which it is almost impossible to keep up with. No doubt, the serious and scientific matter so far published is not beyond the scope of an individual, and the present writer has tried to keep abreast of it from the start, having been in 1947 one of the first to have seen and identified any of the scrolls which had just come to light in Jerusalem.

It has become impossible to keep track of the popular literature on the subject in its entirety, if for no other reason than that one would need to know nearly every language in the world to follow all that has been said on the radio and in newspapers and periodicals. However, this is no great disadvantage, because popular literature draws on, or at least should be drawing on, the scientific publications which are trying to present reliable new knowledge about serious ancient matters.

It seems at present as though the new finds will contribute more to the history of ancient Judaism and early Christianity than to our knowledge of the ancient text of the Bible. Only specialists can appreciate the value of the Old Testament texts, while the general reader will be content to admire Hebrew manuscripts of the Bible which are a thousand years older than any hitherto known, and yet offer the selfsame text for all practical purposes.

But even here enough material was supplied to make scholars' hearts beat faster, and some of them seized the pen to attack each other in a way which it is hard to reconcile with the serenity demanded of the scientific scholar. Worse, however, was to follow when it came to reckoning the contribution of the non-biblical texts to the history of Christian origins. A large number of publications appeared which succeeded in misleading a portion of the public in an irresponsible fashion. Efforts were even made to bring discredit upon scholars who were devoting themselves seriously and dispassionately to the study of the texts, simply because they refused to subscribe to certain views.

The object of this book is to make clear to the reader the significance of the finds, by placing them and explaining them within the framework of the age in which they were composed, and thus letting the ancient documents speak for themselves as far as possible. When we are defining this framework, however, we have to reckon with much that is uncertain and obscure. We have therefore striven to omit, as far as may be, all that is doubtful, and to present what are assured results in their proper light. A book such as this must bear the hallmark of the year in which it was written, since new discoveries are still being made, and publication of the finds has only started.

Nijmegen, 14 November 1956.

J. VAN DER PLOEG, O.P.

I

'THE GREATEST MANUSCRIPT DISCOVERY OF MODERN TIMES'

EAST and south-east of Jerusalem lies the desert of Judah, a desolate landscape that was part of the territory of ancient Judah, one of the twelve tribes of Israel. The region that was allotted to this tribe when the country was divided was by no means the best of the land, and it is not surprising that we know little of the history of Judah in the first centuries of Israel's existence as an independent people in its own country. Only later does it come into prominence, when the tribe had been reinforced by other groups, which it could assimilate because they were akin to it. A great deal of its territory is 'desert': not sand-flats, such as many imagine in a desert, but a waste region almost devoid of plant-life, composed of hills, deep valleys and rocky ravines. In prehistoric times, nature must have kept house here under terrifying conditions. The strata of the hills are tilted sharply, showing a region subject to earthquakes, where subterranean pressures had caused mighty folds and faults, leaving shattered zones of rock in many places.

In the spring, this waste land is covered for a few weeks or months, depending on how much rain has fallen, with a downy translucent green, a desert vegetation where coloured flowers gleam in random patches. For a moment, the visitor ceases to feel, or to believe, that he is in a desert. But if he comes back a short time later, in the month of May, or better still, in June or July, he finds that all this glory has vanished, and if he remembers his Bible, he will be reminded of the texts that speak of the grass that is here today and is gone tomorrow—a symbol of mortality full of meaning for the inhabitants of that land. The wilderness is withered and dead, the heat of the day is almost unbearable as it hangs over the bare rocks and sand-hills, and the air seems to quiver on the ground before the feet of the visitor.

Here and there at the foot of the hills springs of water are to be found, round which, from time immemorial, human dwellings have clustered: villages, which in Palestine and far outside its borders take the form of small, sometimes very small, cities; or again, groups of houses huddled together in untidy blocks. The farther to the east one goes, and the closer one comes to the Dead Sea, the wilder the landscape becomes, till finally all building ceases and the country seems to be uninhabited. But on this last point, the European traveller who visits these regions is constantly mistaken. If he makes a trip through the desert with some companions, and stops somewhere to rest or bivouac, it will not be long till some curious Bedouin turn up to see what is going on. Even here there are inhabitants, and this region could well have been assigned as dwelling-place to one of the twelve tribes.

The Dead Sea is well to the east. While the crest of the mountains of Judah are some 2,500–3,000 feet high, the surface of the Dead Sea lies no less than 1,200 feet *below* sea-level. The desert of Judah slopes down gently at first, broken only by some deep clefts; but once it is near to the inland sea, the land falls sharply to a plateau, which in many places has two levels, a higher and a lower. This plateau runs out to the bright, transparent water of the sea, which mostly ripples softly against its banks as though it had nothing else to do. This is true enough, because its salt content is so high—nearly 25 per cent—that no fish can live in it, men can hardly bathe in it, it cannot be used for irrigation, and only the Palestine Potash Company, once at the mouth of the Jordan, now at the south of the Dead Sea, is trying to exploit it.

Here the Bedouin still live in tribes. Their poor, black tents can be seen grouped together in some few places, and they drive their sheep and goats through the country, where the beasts seem to be constantly devouring the last blade of grass. They speak a dialect of Arabic, their religion is that of Islam. When nearly three thousand years ago David fled here to escape Saul's ambushes, he and his men led a nomad life that cannot have differed much from that of the Bedouin of today. It was sparsely populated then as now, because years passed and Saul could not trap there his former squire and minstrel. At present, one of the best-known tribes of the district is the Taamireh Bedouin, who have gained in recent years a remarkable reputation (and a remarkable income) as the discoverers of the scrolls concealed in the desert.

How did the scrolls come to be there? There is still to be seen by the Dead Sea a settlement which is well known from the Bible and ancient history: Engaddi. It possesses a great spring of fresh water to make life possible. Engaddi lies on the west side of the sea, about half-way between its most northerly and southerly points. A good bit farther to the north, where there is also a spring with fresh enough water, there was already a human settlement in the time of the Jewish monarchy, that is, in the eighth and seventh centuries before Christ. This spring is now called Ain Feshkha. Its water bubbles up in a round pool at the foot of a steep slope, to run down in several streams, through marshy ground, to the Dead Sea a few hundred yards away. A mile or so to the north there was a settlement called in the Bible Ir Ha-melach (Joshua 15: 62), that is, Salt-town. As far as one can say at present, no one lived there for centuries after the great catastrophe of 587, when Jerusalem was destroyed by Nabuchodonosor and a great number of the inhabitants of the country deported. But towards the middle or end of the second century before Christ, Jews came to live there, and occupied it till A.D. 68. Roman soldiers took their place, and withdrew some decades later. From A.D. 132–135, Jewish soldiers made it a strong-point in their war against the Romans, in another desperate effort to drive the hated heathen from the land.

The men who lived here at the beginning of the Christian era left manuscripts behind them. These are the documents that have come to light again since 1947, and they will be the subject-matter of this book.

The story of the first finds, which included the longest and best-preserved of the manuscripts, has been often written, and many readers will know it well. It is recalled here in brief. In the spring of 1947, at the time of year that the rough country is somewhat green, a young Taamireh Bedouin was grazing a flock of black-haired goats in the uplands by the Dead Sea, some eight miles south of Jericho. Goats are obstinate animals that go their own way just when they should not. They are good climbers and perform well over rock, often making it hard for a man to follow them, even a Bedouin. So it happened that while the flock scattered to graze, one of the goats strayed away, and climbed up a rocky path along the wall of rock that runs from north to south along the Dead Sea. A goat-herd ran after it, and came to a sudden stop before a gap in the rocks, which looked like the opening of a cave. Some large jars could be seen inside. The young man thought of hidden treasure. He threw a stone into the cave, and then another. A jar broke, but no gleam of gold or silver appeared. With much effort, he climbed through the gap, and found himself in a natural cave, some eight yards long and nowhere more than six feet wide. Some jars stood there, with fragments of other jars lying about, and large and small pieces of leather on which there was writing. In the jars that were sealed by good lids there were what seemed to be complete rolls, likewise of leather and with writing on one side of it. The rolls were wrapped in linen, which had mostly perished and in some places stuck to the leather like pitch.

Older members of the tribe were told of the find, and the result was that the two jars, with their contents, and some large pieces of leather, not re-rolled but folded, were carried out. The Taamireh were already aware of the fact that in their country the ground could yield objects which men from Europe and America sought, and often paid good money for. They were therefore well pleased with their find, but to have it valued they took it to the Mohammedan elder at Bethlehem. He looked carefully at the writing on the leather rolls, and when he saw that it was not Arabic—the language of the Koran, and therefore the only important one—sent the men to a local dealer in antiquities, a Syrian named Kando. Kando discussed the matter with a colleague at Jerusalem, also a Syrian. The latter informed his bishop, Mar Athanasius Jesus Samuel, Syrian 'Archbishop-Metropolitan of Jerusalem and all Transjordan'.

From this moment the bishop began to play an important role in the affair of the documents. He belongs to the Jacobite branch of the Syrians, a group called after the monk Jacob Baradai who established in the sixth century a Syrian hierarchy of bishops and priests independent of the sees of Rome and Byzantium. He became thereby the founder of an independent Syrian Church, whose position with regard to dogma is that Jesus Christ is really and truly God and truly man, but that it is not proper to speak of two natures *in* Christ, for fear of dividing the one Christ and Son of God. At present the Jacobites form a group of perhaps a hundred thousand among the Christians of the Near East. They are under the authority of a patriarch and have eight or ten bishops. Mar Athanasius is one of these, a man of about forty years of age in 1947, when he was residing in Jerusalem, in a monastery, as the ancient Syrian custom demanded. The monastery was St Mark's, who is called Mar Markos by the Syrians. (Mar means 'lord': as title of a bishop, much the same as the French Monseigneur.) It is supposed to occupy the site of the house of St Mark the evangelist, which was destroyed in A.D. 70. According to the inmates of the monastery, it was in this house that Jesus held the Last Supper. The monastery itself is not impressive. To reach the gate, one must go through a maze of narrow, evil-smelling streets in the south-west corner of old Jerusalem. When admitted, one sees a courtyard, a chapel with a beautiful ancient door of Arabic workmanship, and then all sorts of rooms and corridors built on to each other without much signs of planning. Only a few monks still live there, and the number of Christians over whom the bishop has authority is insignificant. His office is titular rather than real, and his chief function is to represent the Jacobite Church at Jerusalem with pomp and circumstance.

In the block of buildings which form the Church of the Holy Sepulchre, the Jacobites have their own room for the performance of their ceremonies. It is a dark and gloomy cellar, with room for a hundred people, which looks as though it would do better service as a prison than as a sacred place.

The monastery possesses a famous library of Old Syriac manuscripts, which have been studied there by various scholars of Europe. It is not easy to get permission to see them, because most of the Orientals guard their ancient manuscripts as jealously as in past centuries Roman *monsignori* and others guarded the manuscripts and the archives of the Vatican. When Mar Athanasius heard of the discovery of manuscripts in the desert, his interest was aroused at once. They could be an acquisition for his library—or he might be able to sell them advantageously, and so do some very necessary good to the funds of the monastery. He decided to buy them, but to go as circumspectly as possible about the work. Without saying a word to any of his monks, he sent for the dealers in anti-quities, who were members of his flock. They brought with them an ancient leather roll, fawn-coloured and very brittle. The text on it seemed to be Hebrew. The bishop would have been no true Oriental if he had bought the piece at once. He sent the two men home with it, urging them to get hold of the other rolls, which they said were still in the hands of the Bedouin.

Weeks passed, and it was not till the beginning of June that the dealer Kando telephoned his bishop to say that three Bedouin had turned up with the other rolls. The bishop told him to send them on to Jerusalem, and sat down to wait for them. He had great expectations, but informed nobody of what was afoot.

The three men arrived, carrying their treasures. They were dressed, like many desert nomads, in ragged clothes; they had no proper shoes, their beards were untrimmed, and they lacked all the civilized trappings which urban dwellers prize so highly, even in the East. A monk called Boulos met them at the door of the monastery. All he could see was that they were rough and dirty, like their wares, and that the script on their rolls was not in the sacred Syriac which Jesus himself had spoken while on earth. (Jesus spoke Aramaic; Syriac is a later dialect of Aramaic.) He dismissed them on the spot, and they surely parted without the usual expressions of politeness.

During the midday meal, Boulos mentioned the incident to

his bishop, casually, to make conversation. The bishop blenched, recognized that he had blundered, grew angry and rang at once the dealer of Bethlehem to tell him what had happened. Kando had a sad story for him. It appeared that the three Arabs had not left the monastery far behind when they met a Jewish merchant near the Jaffa Gate and offered to sell him the rolls. The merchant wanted to know where they were found and urged the Arabs to come to his place of business to get their money. They hesitated. They probably knew the law of the land, according to which they were forbidden to keep antiquities that they had discovered, or to sell them to a third party. Antiquities belonged to the Government, which could reward the finder by giving him back a portion of the find later on. The cautious procedure of the Jewish merchant had not inspired their confidence, and the upshot was that two of the three Arabs had entrusted their share of the treasure to Kando, while the third had sold his share to the Mohammedan elder of Bethlehem. That was what Kando told the bishop, at any rate. How true it was, no one can say. It is difficult to reconstruct the story of the finds, because there are discrepancies in details. See, for instance, the accounts in the works of Wilson and Allegro mentioned at the end of this book. We know one thing, namely that the third share mentioned above was bought by Professor E. Sukenik, professor of Palestinian archaeology at the Hebrew University of Jerusalem. When the bishop heard the story, he went after the other scrolls, and never rested till he had them in his possession. How much he paid for them was not known till later: apparently a few Palestinian pounds, which were at the time equivalent to sterling. The bishop now says twenty-four.

Thus in early June 1947 the bishop was in possession of his scrolls, five in number, the largest and best-preserved portion of the finds. The remainder came to rest in the Hebrew

University, and was in a much worse condition. The bishop now decided to ask competent advice about the significance and the value of his purchase. The first person he consulted was a Syrian official of the Department of Antiquities, who assured the bishop that it was not worth twopence. The second was the author of this book.

I had in fact known the bishop for some time, as I had paid him a visit twice. The manuscripts of the monastery had interested me, as had the monastery itself, and above all its inmates, the Syrian monks, and their customs. In 1942 I had brought out a book, published by Brill's of Leyden, about ancient Syrian monastic life, and during my first visit to the Near East, from 11 December 1946 to 11 December 1947, I had naturally used the opportunity to make contact with Syrian and other Oriental monks. I stayed at the Dominican Fathers' School of Biblical Studies at Jerusalem, where Arabic was taught by Father S. Marmadji, a Dominican who had formerly been a Catholic priest of the Syrian rite in Iraq. The bishop knew him, and asked him one day to find out from me whether I could read Hebrew manuscripts. I answered that apart from my Old Testament and Syriac studies, I had never worked on them, and that I would have to inspect them to be able to say could I read them or not. When my answer reached the bishop, he invited me to come to the monastery with Father Marmadji and have a look at his Hebrew manuscripts. I decided to go.

In the last week of July (not August, as the bishop mistakenly said in *The Biblical Archaeologist*, May 1949, p. 28) we went together to the monastery, and were brought into the bishop's divan (reception room). Every house in the Near East has such a divan, which is usually the largest room in the house. There were rugs on the floor, some small tables in the middle, and sofas and chairs around the walls. The bishop sat on a chair in one corner, facing the door diagonally. We were given seats beside him, and after the opening Oriental formalities, which were carried on in Arabic and English, of which latter the bishop had some command, a tray was carried in. On it lay four leather scrolls, yellow and brown with age. The bishop announced that they had been found in jars somewhere in the country (he refused to say where) and that they were two thousand years old. The first part of his statement took me by surprise, the latter part left me incredulous. However, I would have a look. I took the largest of the four scrolls, unrolled it with the help of Father Marmadji, and tried to read the script. When the scroll was measured later, it was found to be about a foot wide and twenty-four feet long. But it was not its size that held my attention at the moment. I could see clearly that the text was in Hebrew, but I found the script strange, so that I could not read it fluently at first sight. It was the now famous manuscript which contains the complete book of Isaiah, and as luck would have it, the doctorate thesis which I had presented in Rome thirteen years earlier had dealt with important texts from Isaiah. I still knew these texts well, and when I came upon one of them after some unrolling of the scroll, the thought immediately came to my mind that this could well be an Isaiah manuscript, for use in the synagogue or the like. The place of this text in the book I knew corresponded with its place in the scroll, and having identified one text, I quickly found others which confirmed my conclusions.

With this in mind, I determined to make sure by looking at the beginning of the text and examining the end for a possible colophon (date or other information added by the copyist). With the help of Father Marmadji, I unrolled the document almost completely. But coming near the end, we found the scroll so brittle that bits began to break off. They fell on the floor, and I watched the bishop carefully, to see if he had noticed, as in fact he had. Even the tiniest fragments of an old manuscript are important, and no expert and no responsible librarian would let them be lost. If the bishop had any notion of what it meant to see a two-thousand-year-old manuscript being disintegrated, he must have jumped up and interfered at once. But nothing happened, and I found that strange, if not suspicious. To avoid further damage to a manuscript which did not belong to me, I rolled it up quickly and tried the other end. But there it was just as brittle and so I did not unroll it completely at either end. Taking another good look at the scroll, it seemed to me that there could be little doubt that it was a complete text of Isaiah, no more and no less. But that it was two thousand years old, as the bishop affirmed without offering a single proof, I did not accept.

Then I saw a second scroll, where I thought I discovered a miscellany of biblical and non-biblical texts. The biblical texts which I could read—the whole examination of the scrolls lasted only a short time—seemed to come from one of the minor prophets. This was undoubtedly the commentary on the first two chapters of Habacuc, which was later to become famous. In it the text of the Bible is followed verse by verse by an exposition. There were two other rolls, where I could see that the text was not from the Bible. They were the two portions of what was later recognized as the rule for members of a Jewish sect. The bishop may have had his fifth scroll at the time, but he did not let me see it, presumably because the rolls of leather were stuck together by damp, and it was to a great extent ruined. However, nothing could have been made of it at the moment.

I did not know what to think of the whole affair, but for the time being I was not prepared to accept the incredible age ascribed to the scrolls, as long as the bishop failed to provide any proof of it. The desert sands of Egypt had of course been providing a continuous series of finds of manuscripts and fragments for many years, and I knew that something of the sort had happened in the Near East, though rarely and then only of some fragments. Nothing of the sort had ever happened in Palestine. I wondered for a moment were the texts forgeries, but rejected the idea at once as most improbable. Though I was no expert in the matter and knew of some famous forgeries, it seemed to me that the typically brittle state of the leather, and the obvious antiquity of the scrolls were indubitable proofs of their authenticity. The scrolls I had before me were really ancient: but from what period?

As a step towards verifying the bishop's assertion, I asked him could I put him in touch with the Hebrew University, where I knew some of the scholars. The bishop refused. Perhaps then with someone from the library of ancient Hebrew manuscripts at the Schocken Foundation, where I could easily make contacts? The bishop refused, just as firmly. There was in Jerusalem at the time a Jewish scholar from Amsterdam, who, I thought, considering the position he held, must know his way around ancient Hebrew manuscripts. The bishop agreed to my bringing him over, but when the time came to invite the scholar in question, he could not come. Would the bishop then let us have one of the jars in which as he said the rolls were found? There were experts at the Dominican School who could judge from the form and material of such a utensil the period from which it derived. If the jar was thought to be two thousand years old, there would be still no proof that the manuscripts were of the same date, but for me at least it would be a reason for going into the matter seriously. The bishop promised a jar. With this promise I departed, hoping to hear more of it later. But before leaving, I took a number of photographs of the monastery, the church, the bishop (reproduced in this book) and the monks. The roll of film, on which I took other pictures later, enabled me to date my visit exactly.

When I returned to the Biblical School, I spoke that afternoon of what I had seen. An eminent scholar warned me seriously—and rightly—against a possible forgery. The fact that no archaeologist had ever made such a discovery or even heard of the like, joined to the fact that the bishop positively refused my offer to put him in touch with Jewish scholars from Jerusalem, seemed to indicate almost with certainty that the scrolls were of no importance. The argument impressed me so much that I decided to wait till the jars arrived at the school. But the bishop never made good his promise, for the simple reason that Athanasius Samuel did not have them in his possession when he was speaking to me, and in fact never got possession of them. Professor Sukenik is the lucky person who managed to buy two of them. Nothing is known of any others.

When the pottery failed to arrive, I was confirmed in my conviction that the scrolls were of no significance to me personally and I paid no further attention to the matter. I was of course mistaken, but it was my first time in Palestine— which was not then divided into two States at war with each other—and each day brought so many new impressions with it that the thought of the scrolls of St Mark's monastery was simply squeezed out. Life is like that. It may happen that a person does or omits something, without being able to account for it properly, simply because he did not give the matter his complete attention. He may be sorry later, or wonder how it could have been so, but then it is too late to undo what is done. That is what happened to me.

Later that year I saw the bishop once again. He was away for a long time during the summer, but after a few months I

was able to present him with some of the photographs which
I had taken on my previous visit. He spoke again about the
scrolls, and added that they had been found in a cave in the
desert. Where precisely, he did not say.

In the meantime matters had proceeded as he was later to
narrate in an American periodical. He had left Jerusalem on
5 September 1947, taking the scrolls with him, and had
shown them to his Patriarch, Ignatius Ephraim I, at Homs on
the Orontes. The Patriarch was a learned man, a former
student of the Catholic Seminary of the Dominicans at Mosul,
and author of many works in Arabic, including a history of
Syrian literature. He knew little or no Hebrew, however, and
had as little faith as I myself in the age of the scrolls. He advised
the bishop to talk to the professor of Hebrew at the American
Methodist University of Beirut. The bishop went there on
22 September, but the professor was on vacation, and, like
everyone else who could afford it, had left the unbearable
summer heat and humidity of the city far behind him. So the
bishop returned to his monastery at Jerusalem on 26 September,
without having met anybody who could confirm authorita-
tively his own opinion of the age and value of the scrolls.

He sent once more for the Syrian official from the Department of Antiquities, Stephen Hanna Stephen, asking him to
bring some books. The Syrian continued to maintain that the
scrolls were worthless, and the bishop perused the books
without finding anything to help him. A few days later
Stephen returned, accompanied by a Jewish expert in
antiquities. The expert had a good look at the scrolls, which
were lying on a little table, and then said: 'If that table were a
box, and you filled it full of pound notes, you could not even
then measure the value of these scrolls, if they are two
thousand years old, as you say' (see *The Biblical Archaeologist*,
1949, p. 30: the bishop's own English version). The bishop was

discouraged at getting nothing more definite, but made a good mental note of what was said, as appears from the sequel.

In the beginning of October he had a visit from a Jewish doctor, who had some business to do with him about house property. He showed the doctor the rolls, and asked him his opinion of them. The doctor confessed ignorance, but promised to send someone along without delay who could really say what the scrolls were and what they were worth. On his return home, he got in touch with the president of the Hebrew University, Dr J. L. Magnes, who a few weeks later sent two experts from his library to examine the rolls. They came, looked, departed, and returned no more. Clearly, they had no confidence in the importance of the finds.

No doubt, things would have gone differently if the bishop had put his cards on the table from the start. His secretiveness was due to the fact that he wanted to make the greatest possible profit from his purchase, as also, among other things, to the fact that he did not want to put anyone on the track of the finds, in case there were more discoveries. But meanwhile the Bethlehem dealer, Kando, had found out where the cave lay and had gone there with a helper. The two of them took away all sorts of fragments which the Bedouin had left behind. The bishop probably did not know this when, having himself learned where the cave was, he sent some members of his community there. They found very little, and did all the more damage. To gain easier access to the cave, they made a large hole under the high and narrow entrance, and threw out everything that could be moved in the cave. Any booty they found they brought to their bishop and task-master: a number of fragments from old manuscripts, which he added to his collection.

Not knowing what else to do, Athanasius now took a Syrian merchant named Kiraz into his confidence. In the year 1945,

Kiraz had built a house in Jerusalem, in the quarter called Talpiot, where the digging of the foundations had brought Jewish ossuaries to light—burial-chests containing human bones. The expert in this field was the Professor Sukenik whom we have already mentioned, and Kiraz made his acquaintance on that occasion. Sukenik had now succeeded in getting possession of the manuscripts that the bishop had missed. Kiraz showed him the great Isaiah scroll, which he had obtained from the bishop for a while. Sukenik studied it for a short time, made some notes and then gave it back.

Sukenik is undoubtedly the first person, after Athanasius, who was convinced of the antiquity of the manuscripts. He was one of the few scholars in the world competent to form a judgment at the time. Hebrew manuscripts of pre-Christian date were then unknown. All there was was a piece of papyrus from Egypt, containing mostly the text of the ten commandments. It was known as the Nash Papyrus, and scholars were far from agreement about its date. It was attributed mostly to the second or first century before Christ, or to the first century after Christ. The script is anything but elegant, and looks like the work of someone who seldom took pen in hand and then wrote only with difficulty. There were also a small number of inscriptions, mostly proper names, and a number of *graffiti* on burial-chests, that is, rough scribbles giving the names of the dead whose bones were in the coffins. These *graffiti* are rarely elegant in form. It looks as if the chest was bought ready-made, and that the buyer scratched the name on it himself. Professor Sukenik had made a special study of this branch of Jewish antiquities, and therefore knew how men wrote in Palestine at the turn of the Christian era. The script of the scrolls showed marked resemblance to that of the *graffiti*, etc., and hence he concluded that they must come from the same date.

Unfortunately, Sukenik's discovery came towards the end of 1947, when the British Mandate over Palestine was coming to an end. British troops and administrators were gradually withdrawing, and the country was left to anarchy, where the hostile parties were able to take over on their own initiative the parts of Palestine allotted them by the United Nations. I had personal experience of the free-for-all in the country, and it nearly cost me my life. On 10 December 1947, the Biblical School held its usual monthly excursion, a day trip whose objective this time was Modin, where the Maccabees are buried. We went in taxis driven by Arabs. No one expected danger. One of the drivers had even brought a couple of his children with him, in the luggage compartment. Order was still maintained in Jerusalem, though a state of war existed in the mountains. A few hours out, we were held up by armed Arabs. After long discussions, everything was smoothed out, and we were offered coffee as a token of peace. Further on, however, things did not go so well. When we came to a certain village which we had to leave by the same way that we entered, we found our route barred by armed men, with no retreat possible. The leader of our party, Father Benoît, had to go off in one of the taxis to an Arab committee far away in the hills. We could leave only when we had a safe-conduct from them. Meanwhile we were guarded by a party of men armed with archaic weapons, some of which must have come from the time of Napoleon but which were still lethal. I was convinced that all would be well, but I was due at the Tel Aviv airport early the next morning on my way back to Europe, and in my excitement I stepped out of the group to see if there was any sign of our taxi coming back. Suddenly I heard my name shouted behind me: 'Come back, they're shooting!' Their fingers were on the triggers, and if they had pressed them, I should have been a fatal casualty. Such were the conditions in the Holy Land at the time that Professor Sukenik made the greatest discovery of his life. Under these circumstances, it is hard to blame the bishop for leaving the country with the scrolls some time later, even though this was against the laws which still held good, on paper. The British administration had ceased to function, and there was no other government actually in control.

In February 1948, Athanasius sought contact with the American School of Oriental Research. The director, Professor Millar Burrows, was in Baghdad at the time, and the bishop was received by Dr John C. Trever, a young American who, among other things, was collecting material for lectures on the Bible which he hoped to give in America. The American School is a few minutes' walk from the old city, and the situation was then so strained that it was not easy to reach the monastery from it, as the monastery was inside the old city. However, contact was made, and on Friday, 20 February, a monk from the monastery named Abuna Butros Sowmy rang the bell at the American School, having announced himself the day before. He brought with him five scrolls and a fragment. He said that he had discovered the scrolls himself in the monastery library while cataloguing books. Would Dr Trever give him some information about them? Naturally, he obliged. He was in a better position than I had been seven months before, because he had material under his hand with which to compare the scrolls, a copy of the Nash Papyrus mentioned above. Trever was a young man, and so perhaps somewhat less sceptical about strange discoveries in Palestine than the older critics. He saw a great resemblance to the Nash Papyrus, got permission to photograph the scrolls and dispatched some samples of the Isaiah text to Professor William F. Albright, a brilliant American scholar who is one of the greatest authorities on Palestinian archaeology. An answer came as early as 15 March, by air-mail: 'My heartiest congratulations on the greatest manuscript discovery of modern times. There is no doubt in my mind that the script is more archaic than that of the Nash Papyrus. . . . I should prefer a date around 100 B.C. . . . What an absolutely incredible find! And there can happily not be the slightest doubt in the world about the genuineness of the manuscript.'[1] After this letter, Trever and his partner Dr W. Brownlee had no more doubts, and a new era in the study of the scrolls began.

At that moment, the authorities and the archaeologists did not know who was the Bethlehem dealer who was in touch with the Bedouin. Kando kept quiet. He saw no point in making himself known as the discoveries became world famous and it became common knowledge that treasures had been found in Palestine which the finders, contrary to the laws about the finding of antiques, had sold and even taken abroad. The regulations valid under the British Mandate had been taken over by the Governments of Israel and Jordan, and Kando was very much afraid. He was reached at last in early 1949, as a result of the cautious, skilful and indeed courageous efforts of Joseph Sa'ad, secretary of the Rockefeller Museum at Jerusalem. After lengthy negotiations, after the manner of the Oriental haggling game, Kando was induced to sell a number of fragments which he had in his possession to the Jordan Department of Antiquities. G. L. Harding was then its director, and remained in charge until October 1956. The price was a pound sterling per square centimetre. At this first meeting, Kando got a thousand pounds for a number of dirty and partly ruined fragments of old leather which he had himself bought for only a tiny fraction of that sum. There was a rumour at the time that the bishop, who had meanwhile taken his scrolls to America, was asking a cool million dollars for

[1] *The Bibical Archaeologist,* 1949.

them. I heard the rumour myself at the time, and as in fact he got a quarter of a million dollars for them in the end, the rumour cannot have been far from the truth. It was very good for the price of the fragments as they came in, from the point of view of the finders, but did no good at all to the buyers.

The honour of tracing the cave where the Bedouin had found the scrolls belongs to Captain Lippens, an officer of the Belgian Army, who was acting as observer for the United Nations Palestine Commission. Lippens, a well-to-do Belgian of good family, had in his student days taken a degree at the Oriental Institute of Louvain University. He had read about the scrolls in the newspapers, and he made it a point of honour as a Belgian and a graduate of Louvain to have a hand in the new discoveries. He knew already that the scrolls had been found in a cave near the Dead Sea, and therefore in territory covered by Bedouin tribes. Men from that part of the desert were serving in the Arab Legion, and so Lippens sought contact with the officers of the legion. A Brigadier Ashton was interested, and they were able to identify the cave within a few days.

From this starting-point, scholars and officials of the Department of Antiquities succeeded in reconstructing in part the history of the finds. The reconstruction was necessary, because proof was needed to show that the stories in circulation were based on truth, and that the discovery of two-thousand-year-old manuscripts in the desert was no fable. In addition, there was the hope of linking up with points which might lead to new finds. And this hope came true.

Once the first cave was identified, in January 1949, an official expedition left for it within fourteen days. The leaders were G. L. Harding, director of the Jordan Department of Antiquities, and Father R. de Vaux, o.p., director of the Dominican Biblical School at Jerusalem. They found the cave in a sad state of chaos. Archaeologists go very carefully to work when engaged on excavating and surveying. They take measurements of the terrain continuously, they make photographs of each stage of the investigation, they remove carefully layer by layer all that cannot be left in place, and sift the displaced soil for its contents. At the end of the excavation or sounding they know exactly where every item has come from. Kando, the monks from St Mark's, and their helpers had gone to work quite differently. In their treasure-hunt, they had tossed the soil all over the place, broken through the front wall of the cave, thrown out everything that was not to their liking and then gone away, leaving the confusion at the height to which they had brought it. There is good reason for insisting that all archaeological investigation be done under licence!

Harding and de Vaux found about a thousand tiny fragments of scrolls, which the clandestine investigators had not bothered to take with them. They also found an enormous number of potsherds, the remains of pottery that had once stood in the cave. These were carefully packed and taken to the Rockefeller Museum to be sorted. A number of jars could be reconstructed and it could be determined that there were at least fifty-one of them when they were sound. They also found further portions of the linen in which the scrolls had been originally wrapped, bits of papyrus, a Roman lamp—and a cigarette-roller. Its owner was eventually traced: a certain Jabra, who had formed one of the team sent out by the bishop of St Mark's monastery on illegal excavations. This small detail helped to identify the cave with even greater certainty.

While all this was going on, the Taamirehs were not idle. They knew most of the Judaean desert like the palm of their hand, but they had never explored it for caves. Now they combed the desert for them. They were successful in various places: on the site of the ancient fortress of Hyrcania, which

was later a monastery and is now called Khirbet Mird; in the
Wadi Muraba'at, a good distance south of the first cave; and
finally, in the neighbourhood of the cave itself.

The official archaeologists mostly came too late, but they
did succeed at times in reaching the places where finds had
been made; they were able to buy in some or all of the finds
and even made new discoveries. Thus ten other caves were
discovered near the first. Cave number four is the most
important. The Bedouin found there in 1952 a huge number
of fragments, from a hundred biblical and a few hundred non-
biblical manuscripts. These appear to have been already torn
and damaged in ancient times, and in the centuries that followed dampness, worms, beasts and insects all contributed to
the deterioration of the contents of the cave. The experts were
none the less delighted. They claim that the finds in Cave 4
(8,000 to 10,000 fragments) are even more important than
those of Cave 1, on account of the large number of manuscripts represented. The last cave, number eleven, was found
near Cave 1 at the beginning of 1956. According to our present
information, it contained one relatively complete scroll and a
large quantity of fragments; nothing is yet known of their
contents.

There was an ancient custom of depositing manuscripts in
jars, as we know from ancient writers and from modern
discoveries. We even have accounts of the finding of scrolls in
caves near Jericho! In Mesopotamia, as early as the third
millennium B.C., inscribed tablets were sometimes preserved in
earthenware containers. In 588 B.C., the prophet Jeremiah
gave a contract of sale to his disciple Baruch, bidding him put
it in 'an earthen-ware jar' for safe keeping (Jer. 32: 14). In
Egypt rolls of papyrus were sometimes hidden in jars, of which
a number have been found with their contents. A text from
the time of Rameses III (1198–1166 B.C.) already speaks of this

custom. Many manuscripts have been found in the Near East, which had been placed in jars during the first century before and after the beginning of our era. Lists of them have been drawn up by scholars. The twelve famous codices of the third or fourth century A.D., with their important Gnostic texts in Coptic from the library of Chenoboskion, were also found in an earthenware jar. And so on. The discovery of old manuscripts in jars is therefore nothing unusual. The novelty is that it has now happened in Palestine, where it seemed hitherto unknown.

This last opinion, however, soon proved incorrect, when the scattered pages of the history of Palestine were once more studied. An old story, reported by Bishop Epiphanius of Salamis (fourth century) but hitherto little heeded, tells how in A.D. 217 the so-called Quinta Editio (fifth edition) of the Old Testament in Greek was found in a jar near Jericho, along with other Greek and Hebrew books. The same source tells us that the Sexta Editio (sixth edition) was found in similar circumstances at Nicopolis near Actium on the west coast of Greece. The ecclesiastical writers Eusebius (third–fourth century) and Origen (second–third century) put it the other way round, and say that the Sexta was found near Jericho, the Quinta near Nicopolis. But the three testimonies prove conclusively that Greek and Hebrew books were found in jars in the neighbourhood of Jericho. A new light has been thrown on the fact by the finds of 1947.

But that is not all. The German Orientalist J. Fück called the attention of Professor O. Eissfeldt of Halle, an Old Testament scholar, to a translation of a Syriac letter, published in the first volume of the periodical *Oriens Christianus*. The letter was written by the Nestorian Patriarch Timothy I (780–823) and was addressed to Sergius, Metropolitan of Elam and one of the most important prelates in the Nestorian

Church. The Patriarch resided at Seleucia-Ctesiphon (a double city, no longer existing, on the Tigris not far south of Baghdad) and wrote as follows:

> . . . We learn from trustworthy Jews, who have recently received instruction in the Christian doctrine, that books were found near Jericho ten years ago, in a house in the rocks. They say that an Arab's dog was hunting an animal, pursued it into a cave and did not come out. Its master went after it and found in the rock a little house that contained many books. The huntsman then went to Jerusalem and told it to the Jews. Many of them then went out and found books of the Old Testament, along with others, in the Hebrew script. And because my informant knew the script and was himself a Scribe, I asked him about some texts which are quoted in our New Testament as coming from the Old, but which are found nowhere in the Old Testament, either as read by us or by the Jews. He said to me: they are to be found in the books that were found there. And as I had heard this from the catechumens, and as I had asked others and received always the same answer, I wrote about it to the noble Gabriel, and also to Shuvalemaran, Metropolitan of Damascus. . . .

Timothy goes on to say that more than two hundred psalms of David had been found among the books! His letter is unfortunately not dated. The incident of which it speaks probably took place shortly before 800. It resembles so closely what happened in 1947, and the discoveries correspond so exactly to what came out of the modern incident, that a number of scholars think that there is some connexion between them. It seems clear that there were earlier finds in the district south of Jericho, not far from the Dead Sea, where the caves with manuscripts are so numerous. Just as now, Hebrew and Greek texts of the Old Testament and other books were found, among which are a number of psalms not found in the Bible. Only one item of the information given to Timothy is suspect, and that not entirely: that texts were found of an unusual type, which agreed with quotations from the Old Testament in the New. (As is well known, the Old Testament sometimes appears to be quoted rather inexactly in the New, or at least in a form which differs from the known texts of the Old Testament. This is an ancient problem, for which various solutions have been offered which are irrelevant here; the Patriarch Timothy was looking for a solution in his day.) Timothy appears to have been given a very general assurance, but not the texts themselves. The catechumens, in the true Oriental way, probably gave the patriarch the answer that they knew he was looking for. Gabriel and the bishop of Damascus could not possibly have verified it. Since 1947 the new biblical texts have shown departures (in minor details) from the texts we knew. Texts may yet be found which agree with the quotations in the New Testament, and it may be that such were found in the time of Timothy.

Once attention was fixed on famous old stories about finds of biblical manuscripts in caves, more were remembered. There still exists among the Jews a sect called the Karaites. There are not many of them, because most of them lived in the Crimea, where they were nearly exterminated by the invaders during the Second World War. Their name means 'men of the Bible', which is why they are also called *Bnê miqra*, 'sons of the scriptures'. The sect must have been formed in the last part of the eighth century A.D., in Mesopotamia, from which it spread in all directions. Before the last war their numbers were reckoned as about twelve thousand. They are now only a few thousand at the very most. Some scholars hold that the Palestinian Karaites must be linked up with the find of Hebrew manuscripts related by the Patriarch Timothy, because Karaite views and customs often reflect those contained in the manuscripts found in 1947. Further, the tenth-century

Karaite Kirkisani speaks of an earlier sect, called 'the men of the caves' because their sacred books had been discovered in a cave. A twelfth-century Karaite also mentions them, while Kirkisani's authority was a famous Karaite who lived about A.D. 900. The Karaites are known as 'the men of the Bible' because they confined themselves to Sacred Scripture and the precepts contained therein, while they rejected the traditions of the rabbis as contained in the Talmud, etc. Hence some scholars think it possible that the Karaites were the people most interested in the finds at Jericho in A.D. 800, since the sect would have preferred ancient Bibles to the texts upheld by the rabbis. Spellings peculiar to the ancient texts are said to have influenced the modern pronunciation of Hebrew.

Professor S. Sergert of Prague has recently called attention to another story from Karaite sources, which is found in a letter written some time before A.D. 961. The author of the letter is Chasdai Ibn Shaprut of Cordova, the recipient is the king of the Chazars, an East European people of Ugric blood, some of whom, with their king, had gone over to Judaism about A.D. 750. The letter had been known for a long time, but it contained, as Sergert pointed out, a tradition recalled by Chasdai, to the effect that a Jew in the highlands of Seïr (in the south of Palestine) had discovered books in a cave, at a spot where other Jews had been accustomed to meet for prayer in the morning and the evening.

To sum up. Since 1947 three places in the desert of Judah have yielded important manuscripts: one to the north of the spring of Feshkha; a second south-west of this in the Wadi Muraba'at; a third near Khirbet Mird, the ancient fortress of Hyrcania, where in A.D. 492 a Greek monastery was founded by Mar Saba. In the first district, the remains of an old building have been found and excavated. The investigations showed that the inhabitants had to do with the caves where the manuscripts were found. The natives call the ruin Khirbet Qumran, and we shall discuss it in detail later on. Khirbet is the Arabic for a hill with ruins on it, or for ruins alone, where they project partly above the ground.

The Wadi Muraba'at was inhabited by Jews in the second century A.D., and they were particularly active there between 132 and 135, the time of the second Jewish revolt. Khirbet Mird has been explored by a Belgian expedition under Professor R. de Langhe, of Louvain and Nijmegen. The remains of an ancient Christian monastery have yielded fragments of Greek biblical texts of the Old and New Testaments, which were written between the fifth and the eighth century. Previous to this, Bedouin had found Greek biblical texts which they said came from the Wadi en-Naar, a southerly prolongation of the valley of the Cedron. This was, however, a deliberate misdirection, given out in the hope of concealing the true source of their finds, with an eye to further discoveries and more personal profit. Khirbet Mird has also yielded some Syro-Palestinian and Arabic texts, and even a sixth-century fragment of a classical tragedy, the *Andromache* of Euripides. This item shows how monks living in the desert far from civilization could still hold classical culture in high esteem. The Greek biblical texts come from the library of the sacred books which they used in church and cloister. Syro-Palestinian is the language they spoke, and which they used in the liturgy along with Greek, until it was eliminated by Arabic. The three sites have nothing to do with one another, but since the last two, which are not on the Dead Sea, have also given us important documents, it is more exact not to speak of the 'Dead Sea Scrolls'. 'Manuscripts from the Judaean Desert' would be better. It has been remarked that 'Dead Sea Scrolls' is incorrect in any case, because the scrolls were not found *in* the Dead Sea but beside it. This, however, is somewhat far-fetched. Many continue to speak of the 'Dead Sea Scrolls' because the expression has become international, and because it is an acknowledged convention of language to speak of something by naming its most important part. And the finds by the Dead Sea are far and away the most important of all that have been discovered in the desert of Judah. The finds in the Wadi Muraba'at are also important for many reasons, for one thing because they include documents signed personally by Bar Kochba, the leader of the second revolt, which may well be called a sensational discovery. The documents from Khirbet Mird appear so far to be relevant above all to the study of the history of Greek Bible translation.

We do not know whether manuscripts or fragments have been found outside the three places mentioned, but it is not impossible. The Bedouin are reluctant to give the bearings of their 'Treasure Islands', and documents have been on sale of which the place of origin was never divulged. The story of the finds in the desert of Judah has impressed on us the fact that one never knows.

2

THE HISTORICAL BACKGROUND

THE previous chapter told how important manuscripts were found by the Dead Sea, and how they became world famous. This chapter could continue the story of the finds, discussing each item in detail and giving a general view of the debates which followed among scholars and amateurs. Our procedure will be different. It is generally agreed that enough definite results have emerged from the study of the texts to allow us to place the texts as a whole in a broad historical setting. From the non-biblical texts in particular, we can tell that the community responsible for the Dead Sea Scrolls was a sort of Jewish brotherhood or sect which to some extent shared the destinies of the Jewish people in Palestine, no doubt during the last three centuries before the Jewish temple was destroyed by Titus in A.D. 70. This will be demonstrated in the following chapters. In the course of the exposition, we shall go into the various questions which arise from one aspect or other of the discoveries, so that the reader will finally be able to form an idea of the whole sequence of events and their significance.

This method is not without its difficulties. The manuscripts have been only partially published and studied up to the present. The historical allusions that crop up in them are to a great extent obscure, and have given rise in each case to widely divergent explanations. Historical reconstruction is, therefore, in many respects a gamble. We must, however, sometimes

take risks. Only in the eyes of the timorous is it supreme
wisdom to undertake nothing until they are absolutely sure of
the outcome. In the type of investigation to which we are
coming, there is one thing to be avoided at all costs. Personal
opinions and hypotheses should not be put forward as certainties, above all, not in popular works destined for the general
public. Unfortunately, in the matter of the Dead Sea Scrolls,
this principle has been much sinned against. The names of
some scholars, happily only a few, and of a large number of
the unlearned, could be mentioned in this connexion. The
present writer has tried to give as objective a picture as possible
of the matter, though he knows that it is not easy, and that it
is impossible to do justice to the views of all learned readers. In
the following historical reconstruction, he has confined
himself in the main to what is gradually being accepted as
solidly proven. Where there is little or no certainty, he will
say so.

Even the essentials are unfortunately still disputed. The
American scholar Solomon Zeitlin, who is one of the lucky
few who have a whole periodical at their disposal to give
world-wide publicity to their views, still maintains that the
scrolls are neither so old nor authentic as is generally admitted.
According to Zeitlin, they are either forgeries, or texts only a
few centuries old, from the Middle Ages at best, and therefore
valueless for the study of ancient Jewish history. He maintains
his opinion, with no little heat, in a growing series of articles
and publications. To put the finishing touches to a number of
earlier articles, he published one of fifty-eight pages in 1950,
with the title: 'The Hebrew Scrolls: once more and finally',
Jewish Quarterly Review, XLI, 1950–51, pp. 1–58. The 'finally'
did not prevent his publishing at least twelve more articles in
the same periodical and a whole book on the subject. Then,
while most scholars agree that the authors and copyists of the

Dead Sea texts belonged to the group of Jews known historically as the Essenes, others will have none of it. One author
actually filled no less than eighty-three pages of a learned
periodical to prove that they were not Essenes. One scholar
of international repute felt bound to conclude, from the
grammatical and other peculiarities of the texts, that they
were only from the Early Middle Ages. So far he has not
retracted. A scholar in England raises a lone voice to say that
the authors and copyists of the texts were not Jews but
Jewish Christians. He has advanced this view in a long series
of articles in a periodical of which he was for many years
editor-in-chief. He seems to have found neither encourage-
ment nor support. Others again have made onslaughts on the
scholars who were acute and courageous enough to set a date
for the texts by their script. These dates were later confirmed
by other lines of research and new discoveries, but so far their
opponents have, to the author's knowledge, made no *amende
honorable*. Others again have claimed that the Dead Sea texts
clearly demand a radical 'rethinking' of some doctrinal
positions of Christianity. With a few strange exceptions, no
one who knows the texts well agrees with this. What matter,
answers another, anyone who does not agree is thereby
branded as a theologian who sees his position endangered and
therefore prefers not to recognize the truth, or at least refuses
to impart it clearly and unambiguously to the layman! So
A. P. Davies, *The Meaning of the Dead Sea Scrolls* (1956)
pp. 82 ff. Be wary of theologians!

What is the ordinary reader to think of all this? That the
scholars have lost their senses and are not to be trusted?
That the subject admits of no certainties, and that science is
helpless where one cannot see for oneself? That the ordinary
reader just cannot follow, and would do better to wait for
twenty-five years, till the smoke of battle has cleared? Or is

he to lose confidence in this kind of research, and give up all
hope of assured results?

In some branches of study, we constantly come upon
practitioners who do not go calmly and objectively to work,
and who do not use the most exact method available, in a
matter where perfect precision is unattainable. They use their
talents, and above all their talents as writers, to make a plaus-
ible case for what they wish to think at the moment. For such
men, a sober and dispassionate study of facts and truth is
sometimes difficult. If this is true of many who are looked on
as scholars, it is still more true of the dilettantes and pseudo-
scholars, who are so numerous precisely in this field. Under
these circumstances, one can see how differences of opinion or
contradictions in the interpretation of the texts from the Dead
Sea may obscure the truth a while for some, but that it is
nevertheless clearly recognizable. Archaeologists of repute
have made mistakes in this field, but have confessed them.
Some, for instance, thought at first that the jars in which the
scrolls were found were from the Hellenistic, not the Roman
period. This led them to date the jars at least a century too
early, which again influenced the dating of the scrolls. But
these specialists were the first to recognize their mistake, and
their retractation did credit both to themselves and to scientific
research, since it showed clearly that their only interest was
the truth. Others, however, having once proclaimed their
opinions in public have remained immovable, even after it had
become clear to everybody that they were wrong. These have
clouded the issue and have given outsiders the impression that
all was confused or hopeless. In the following pages the reader
will find a general picture of how things stand, and on many
points the assured results which are well on their way to being
generally accepted by the scholars who have specialized in the
texts. The writer is not trying to force on the reader his own

personal view, much less a partisan standpoint. Of his impartiality the reader must be judge.

The religious life of Israelites and Jews has displayed a great variety of characteristics all through the history of the people, in biblical times as today. The formation of groups which held themselves more or less aloof from the rest of the people was not unknown even in Old Testament times. The so-called 'sons of the prophets' who appear under Samuel and Saul, that is, as early as 1000 B.C., formed a well-defined group which had its own way of life, though its doctrines were no different from that of the rest of Israel. And when Israel abandoned the cult of Yahweh, or corrupted it by foreign additions, they were on the whole the most zealous champions of the God of the patriarchs. In the time of Jeremiah (round 600 B.C.) and even earlier, there were the Rechabites, an itinerant clan that drank no wine, lived in tents, possessed no fields or vineyards, and so preserved the way of life prescribed by their ancestor (Jer. 35). Their fidelity to their ancestral customs was held out by Jeremiah as an example to the men of Judaea. The priests and the levites also formed a special group in Israel. During the exile, which ended officially in 539 B.C., this group developed strongly under its own hierarchy. In the Psalter we constantly hear the voice of the pious proclaiming that they are beset by godless enemies. Some exegetes are inclined to think that this points to the formation of groups or parties, either before or after the exile, or both. That the pious were organized into groups before the exile does not seem likely, because all traces are lacking in the pre-exilic books of the Old Testament. Things were different in the last centuries before our era.

At the beginning of the second century before Christ, Palestine came under the rule of the Hellenistic monarchy of Syria, whose kings resided at Antioch on the Orontes. Before this, for over two centuries, the Jews had been under Egyptian rule, which had been very tolerant towards the Jews and their religion. Relations were so good that many Jews emigrated to the land of the Nile and founded an important Jewish colony at Alexandria. Conditions changed in Palestine when the Seleucids, the Syrian adversaries of the Egyptian kings, became masters of the land.

There were at the time pious Jews in Israel, called *hasidim* (plural of *hasid*, meaning pious), who tried to regulate their whole life by the prescriptions of the Law of Moses. The Law for them was the expression of the will of God, and was to be observed in every detail and as exactly as possible, in a spirit of entire submission to God's will. How serious they were, how far removed from mere outward legal show, is proved by the fact that such pious men let themselves be killed on the sabbath rather than bear arms to defend themselves against their enemies, believing as they did that to bear arms would be to violate the sabbath rest (I Maccabees 2: 37 f.). This was under Antiochus IV (175–164 B.C.), a classical example of anti-Semitism.

When this king came to the throne he determined to introduce Greek culture and religion into Judaea. Elsewhere he had done that easily, because other peoples could simply add Greek gods and customs to their own. The three centuries before Christ were for the peoples of the Near East the Hellenistic Age, during which took place a large-scale mixture of Eastern and Western (predominantly Greek) institutions and beliefs, diverse in origin but held together by the Greek language and culture. Antiochus was simply a representative of this Hellenism, a child of his age, who felt himself called to take an active part in the development of this culture throughout his realms. Political aims also played their part, and he undoubtedly had before his mind some such motto as 'One kingdom, one ruler, one culture and one religion.' Motives are often mixed and even the politician who never loses sight of his political aims can have cultural ends for which he sincerely strives.

When Antiochus started to put his ideas into practice in Judaea, he met with difficulties which he had not known elsewhere. The Jews were not a people to allow themselves to be ranked with others. What non-Jews thought of them is given apt expression in the book of Esther, where the Persian Haman, their would-be exterminator, speaks as follows to King Xerxes: 'There is a certain people that lives dispersed and isolated among all the peoples in all the provinces of your kingdom. Their laws are different from those of other men and the laws of the king they do not keep. It does not profit the king to let them be' (Esther 3: 8).

The attitude of the Jews towards the Gentile world is well described by the author of the *Epistle of Aristeas*, a Jewish document composed in Greek in the second century before Christ. In it the high priest of Jerusalem criticizes the philosophy of the Greeks and the idolatry of the heathens, and then he is made to say:

> Why should we waste more words on the other foolish peoples, the Egyptians and the like? They place their confidence in beasts . . . they adore them and make them offerings. Now the law-giver considered all these things in his wisdom, because God granted him insight into all things. And He surrounded us with an impregnable rampart and with iron walls so that we should have nothing in common with any other people, but that pure in body and soul, and free from the folly of unbelief, we should revere the one and mighty God above all creatures (*Letter of Aristeas*, 138–139).

The religious leaders of Israel never failed to impress upon the people that they should hold themselves apart from all others. The command is given its strongest expression in the book of Deuteronomy, a work that seems to have received its present form in the last century of Israel's kings (before 600 B.C.) though the kernel of its legislation is much more ancient. This aloofness was beneficial to religion, but created difficulties in social relations, above all when Israel lived in the midst of heathens or under their rule. A segregated life is never pleasant and is rarely profitable. Men in high position, the richer and the more cultured people, feel the burden most.

When Antiochus Epiphanes decided to introduce Greek customs and pagan religious practices into Jerusalem and Judaea, he found allies in 'enlightened' Jews—to use the modern word—who were ready to go some distance with him and to compromise on the strict demands of the Law of Moses. This would enable them to meet others on equal terms and take part in their social life. Antiochus could count on them, and went ahead with his plans. They worked so well that Greek customs and sacrifices to Greek gods were systematically introduced among the Jews of Jerusalem and Judaea, though the worship of Yahweh was not excluded. Numbers of the wealthier classes, numbers even of the priestly aristocracy joined in, followed by large numbers of the type that is always eager to conform to the powers that be. But pious Jews were horrified, and a spectacular incident fired them to express their resentment by open revolt. In the city of Modin, a certain Jew came forward to flaunt his apostasy by offering public sacrifice in the pagan manner. The aged priest Mathathias killed him at the altar, and then fled to the mountains with his sons and his supporters. The revolt gathered strength, and Mathathias' sons took over the leadership in a struggle which they waged with mixed success at first but finally carried to a triumphant conclusion. Antiochus' first reactions were political. They included the abrogation of the Law of Moses, a measure which had not been part of his original plans. Later he sent an army, and went so far as to suppress the cult of the God of the Jews in the temple of Jerusalem. He offered sacrifice to Zeus in the shrine of Yahweh, to the horror of all who loved the God of Israel.

The story of the revolt is told in the two books of Maccabees: in the first, vividly and realistically; in the second, with rhetorical sweep and feeling. (Maccabees belongs to the Bible according to the Catholic, but not the Protestant canon.) Three of the five brothers led the fight one after another, Judas, Jonathan and Simon; two others died heroes' deaths in battle. The three leaders died eventually at the hands of assassins. The last of them, Simon (142–135 B.C.), succeeded in making Judaea completely independent of Syria. In the second year of his leadership the Jews proclaimed him high priest, commander-in-chief and prince, with the right to pass on his dignities to his heirs. Thus he became the founder of a new dynasty which is called the Hasmonaean after the ancestor of the clan. The Hasmonaeans were in a peculiar position, when viewed from the standpoint of the Law and the Prophets. They were not of the kingly race of David, nor did they belong to the legitimate line of high priests. (The Law prescribed that the high priesthood should pass from eldest son to eldest son in the family of Aaron.) Simon's backers knew this very well, but they felt that the times called for his appointment. Besides, provision had been made that the office should last only 'until a faithful prophet appear', that is, till a supernatural intervention brought about a change.

Many, however, must have looked on the situation with disfavour from the beginning. Their resentment grew as the Hasmonaeans began to lead lives of worldly luxury and ceased to feel that there was anything provisional or abnormal in their position. Soon they were behaving like Oriental despots,.

committing acts of injustice and becoming more and more
estranged in spirit from the pious and zealous upholders of the
Law. The party of the Pharisees, which had been formed
among the stricter Jews, broke with the Hasmonaeans under
Simon's successor, his third son, who is known to history by
his Greek name, John Hyrcan (135–104 B.C.). Pharisees and
Hasmonaeans were at enmity with each other till the reign of
Queen Alexandra (76–67 B.C.).

Meanwhile Syria had grown strong again, and we know
that John Hyrcan, in the first six years of his reign, was entirely
under its dominion. The very year that he came to the throne,
Antiochus Sidetes invaded the country, laid it waste, and
besieged Hyrcan in his stronghold of Jerusalem. After enduring a long siege which caused terrible sufferings, Hyrcan had
to capitulate. The unfavourable conditions imposed on him
included even the razing of the walls of the city.

When Antiochus was succeeded by the weak Demetrius II,
Hyrcanus not only regained his independence but was able to
extend his kingdom by conquest in all directions, so that it
was larger than it had ever been under any king of Judah after
Solomon. He built up an army of mercenaries for the purpose,
and his whole behaviour was that of a secular prince, much to
the scandal of the pious.

The mentality of Hyrcan's family was amply demonstrated
by his son Aristobulus. Hyrcan's dying dispositions had been
that Aristobulus was to be high priest and that his widow
was to rule the country. But the son was not content with the
high priesthood. According to Josephus, he threw his mother
into prison, where he let her die of hunger, seized his brothers
and murdered one of them. He finally took the title of king,
which his predecessors had not claimed. Some historians
think that Aristobulus has been painted too black, as the picture
comes from his enemies. There is less doubt unfortunately

about his brother Alexander Jannaeus, who succeeded him
when he died after a year's reign.

Alexander Jannaeus, or Jannai (103–76 B.C.) was a worldling
through and through. He was a fierce warrior who not only
wanted to have his troops at the ready but was determined
to use them, and he was prepared to create a pretext for
waging war if he was not offered one. He pursued this course
all his life, with varying success. Unpopular with the pious,
he had frequently to face widespread and sometimes pro-
longed hostility from his own people. The story is told that
he was once pelted by the crowd with the citrons which they
had brought for the feast and procession, while he was func-
tioning as high priest at the feast of Tabernacles. He is said to
have slaughtered six thousand Jews in revenge. He had to
wage war with the help of foreign soldiers against his own
people. The civil war lasted six years, and cost the lives of
fifty thousand Jews. Finally he invited his opponents to a
parley to end the struggle. They demanded his head and
called in the Syrians. But when they came and met with
success, a remarkable thing happened. When Alexander was
defeated by the Syrians, the national pride of their Jewish
allies was aroused. Six thousand of them who had fought
against Alexander now went over to him, because they
preferred after all to live under a Jewish tyrant rather than
under a heathen king.

With his new helpers and the rest of his earlier army
Alexander inflicted several defeats on his Jewish opponents.
Having finally gained the upper hand, he held a victory
banquet at Jerusalem, to which he invited his concubines, and
crucified eight hundred of his captives before their eyes.
While his victims were still alive, he slaughtered their wives
and children in their presence. This comes from Flavius
Josephus, and the story cannot be checked from other sources.

Josephus adds that Alexander's opponents were so terrified by this gruesome deed that eight thousand of them fled the country by night and did not return as long as he was alive. After this feat of arms, which must have taken place about 88 B.C., Alexander resumed his wars of conquest with fresh courage, striving to eliminate Greek culture, and to introduce the Jewish way of life into the conquered regions. In the last three years of his life he suffered from an illness brought on by heavy drinking. He was buried with great pomp at Jerusalem, after a life as priest and prince that had flouted all the ideals of the pious.

Alexander made over his realm to his wife Alexandra, who ruled for nearly ten years (76–67 B.C.) during which her eldest son Hyrcan II was high priest. To keep the peace and mollify the Pharisees, she gave their customs and casuistry the force of law.

After her death the obvious successor was her son the high priest Hyrcan. But his brother Aristobulus II had other ideas. Raising an army, he took Hyrcan prisoner and forced him to abdicate the royal and the high-priestly power in his favour, while allowing him his income. Hyrcan settled down contentedly to wait for better times, which were not long in coming. Under pressure from those who expected little personal gain from the strong government of Aristobulus, he challenged his brother's rule. At the suggestion of Antipater, father of the Herod who was later to be king, he fled to Petra and allied himself with the king of the Nabataeans, Harith (Aretas). Then the allies marched against Aristobulus and besieged him in Jerusalem.

The Romans now appeared on the scene. The Jews already knew them, and the Romans knew the Jews, even those of Judaea. The Maccabean Judas had made a pact with them, and renewed it on a later occasion. John Hyrcan had done the same at the beginning of his reign. Jews and Romans were therefore officially friends and allies (1 Maccabees 8: 21; 12: 3–4). But the friendship has not gone beyond words, even though these had been inscribed on a bronze tablet and hung up publicly in Rome. The Romans, as a great power, reserved the right to ignore Jewish affairs except in so far as they affected their own national interests. Under Aristobulus the moment was slowly approaching when the Romans were to appear in Judaea, not as allies, but as conquerors.

Long before Aristobulus, the Jews knew well the character of the Romans. This is how the author of the first book of Maccabees (about 100 B.C.) introduces them:

The wars they had waged were recounted [to Judas Maccabeus] and their exploits among the Gauls: how they had conquered this people and made them tributary; all they had done in Spain to gain possession of the gold-mines and the silver-mines of the country; how they had conquered the whole land thanks to their shrewdness and persistence, distant though it was. So too the kings who had come against them from the ends of the earth, crushing them and inflicting great losses upon them, while the others had to pay annual tribute. They had defeated Philip, and Perseus king of the Kitians, and all who had risen against them, and brought all under their sway. Antiochus the Great, king of Asia, had advanced against them with a hundred and twenty elephants, with cavalry, chariots and a great army, and had been defeated by them. They had captured him alive, and imposed on him and his successors a heavy tribute, forcing him to give hostages and to cede territory, including India, Media and Lydia and some of his best lands, which they took from him and gave to king Eumenes. Then, when the people of Greece had determined to march and destroy them, the Romans, hearing of the plan, sent one single general to make war on them, inflicted heavy casualties on them, took their women and children captive, pillaged their possessions, conquered their country, destroyed their fortresses and reduced them to subjection, as they still are to this day. As for the other kingdoms and islands that resisted them, the Romans had crushed them and subjected them to their rule.

But with their friends and supporters they maintained friendly relations. Thus realms near and far are subject to them, and their name strikes terror into all that hear it. Their power is so great that their favour makes kings, and their decree unseats them. In spite of this, none of them has ever worn the royal crown or donned the purple to enjoy its grandeur. But they have set up a council, where three hundred counsellors deliberate continually on all that concerns the people, to direct it prosperously. Every year they give one man power to rule them and to govern the whole country, and this one man is obeyed by all, with no envy or jealousy among them (1 Maccabees 8: 2–16).

This description obviously contains some inaccuracies, but they are understandable, since it reflects the opinion in Palestine before the Romans had appeared there. The Jews knew of Rome's greatness, but there were other lessons to be learnt, which the Jews were to learn the hard way.

In the year 66 B.C. the Roman general Pompey began his triumphal march through the Near East. In 66 he conquered Mithridates VI, king of Pontus in Asia Minor. Tigranes VI of Armenia was terrified into submission. In 65 he sent his legate Scaurus to Damascus in Syria, where he heard of the war in Judaea. Envoys soon arrived from Hyrcan and Aristobulus, and each of the brothers bid for the legate's favour with money. Scaurus took Aristobulus under his wing and commanded Aretas to lift the siege of Jerusalem. In 63 Pompey himself reached Damascus, and at the same moment no less than three Jewish parties presented themselves: Hyrcanus, Aristobulus and a delegation from the people. These last begged Pompey to abolish the Hasmonaean monarchy, which had outlived its usefulness, and to restore priestly rule in Judaea. Pompey counselled calm and patience till he had conquered the Nabataeans, when the parties should have his decision.

Aristobulus had not the patience asked for, aroused Pompey's suspicions by his behaviour, and fled when measures were being taken against him. At first apparently he wanted to fight it out, but thought better of it in time, and when Pompey reached Jerusalem in 63 B.C. he was allowed to enter without opposition, not as ally but as conqueror. But he was still outside the great citadel of the temple, where Aristobulus' supporters had entrenched themselves, determined that the Romans would enter only over their dead bodies. The temple area, fortified by mighty walls, and occupying a hill isolated from its surroundings by ravines, could be taken only by siege, and resisted Pompey for three months. To the indignation and horror of the priests and all pious Jews, the heathen general entered the temple itself, where only priests were allowed. Then his curiosity took him to the shrine accessible to the high priest alone, the holy of holies, of which so many strange rumours were then circulating in the world. To his great disenchantment, he found there only an empty space.

Thus in 63 B.C. the Jews came under the Romans and once more ceased to be masters in their own land. Their independence was restored in part for two brief periods, during the revolts of A.D. 66–70 and A.D. 132–135. Not till 1948 was it fully regained. In 63 B.C. Palestine was made part of the Roman province of Syria, or at least placed under the proconsuls of this province. Hyrcanus was deprived of the title of king, and later had even to confine himself to the duties of high priest. The land was divided into five districts, one of which was centred on Jeruslaem and another on Jericho, each under a Jewish council. But no peace came to the unhappy land. Rival claimants tried to seize the throne by force, the Romans plundered the treasures of the temple, and the Roman civil war, which began in 49 B.C., had repercussions on Judaea. When Pompey was killed in 48 B.C. Hyrcan and Antipater sided with Julius Caesar, who remained grateful to the Jews to the day of his death for the support they lent him everywhere. Hyrcan was rewarded for his loyalty with the title of Prince of the Jews, while Antipater was made governor of Judaea, a post which gave him power over Jews and non-Jews. Under the Romans, he was the real ruler of the land. He gave his sons Phasael and Herod charge of Judaea and Galilee.

Caesar was assassinated in 44 B.C. The Parthians, who now appear for the first and last time in Jewish history, took advantage of the ensuing disturbances to invade Judaea and hold it for three years. They deposed and imprisoned Hyrcan, and amputated his ears to make it impossible for him to exercise any priestly functions: no doubt they had been informed that the Jewish law required a priest to be free from all blemish or mutilation. Antigonus, the son of Hyrcan's brother and opponent Aristobulus, was proclaimed king, and reigned from 40–37 B.C., when he was expelled by Herod.

Herod, nominated king by the Romans, reigned from 37 to 4 B.C. Posterity gave him the name of 'the Great', not for any nobility of character, but because he was energetic—as energetic as he was unscrupulous—and because he built up a great kingdom which he ruled with a firm hand, and which he adorned with great buildings. Sacred Scripture knows him as the author of the massacre of the innocents at Bethlehem.

After the death of Herod his son Archelaus became ruler, though without the title of King, over Judaea, Samaria and Idumaea. His graceless reign was ended in A.D. 6, when he was deposed and banished by the Romans, at the request of the Jews. The land became a Roman province, and remained so from A.D. 6 to 41 then from A.D. 44 to 66, and from A.D. 70 on. Agrippa was king from A.D. 41 to 44, and the great revolt broke out in A.D. 66, which led to the capture of Jerusalem and the destruction of the temple in A.D. 70. That was the end of Jewish independence, except for a brief revival during the revolt of Bar Kochba, which lasted from 132 to 135 and was put down as violently as the first. After that the Jews were forbidden to live in Jerusalem or Judaea, Jerusalem was given the name of Aelia Capitolina and became a Roman colony.

The above outline is in place here, because some knowledge of Jewish history is called for if one is to understand how the brotherhood which wrote the Dead Sea Scrolls came to be and what conditions it lived under. It is the confused and tormented history of an age of crisis, the age also in which Christianity was born. The breakdown of spiritual unity contributed to the confusion. Groups and parties were not merely differentiated, they were in mutual conflict; those who were called to leadership put personal gain above the common good. Kingship and power seemed to some claimants the highest possible aim, to which they sacrificed the interests of the nation and the lives of thousands. The tendency to form parties was stronger than before the exile, and the number of groups with their own peculiar way of life was on the increase. In these trying times the longing for the age of bliss foretold by the prophets grew steadily stronger. Since most of the pious felt themselves impotent to bring about a change, they set all their hopes on a divine intervention which would destroy all evil-doers, Jew and heathen alike, and set up God's kingdom on earth among God-fearing Israelites.

Our knowledge of the parties then existing in Israel was derived hitherto from the New Testament, from some ancient writers and from apocryphal (religious, non-biblical) literature. One of the most important results of the discoveries in the desert of Judah is that we now know more about one particular movement or group, accounts of which had been meagre before. From the Jewish writer Flavius Josephus, whose real name was Joseph ben Mathathias (born A.D. 37, died some time after 105), we knew that at least three groups existed among the Jews in the last period of the second temple, the Pharisees, the Sadducees and the Essenes. We are familiar with the first two from the New Testament. The exact meaning of the word 'Pharisee' is disputed, a little pedantically. Literally it means something like 'separated'. But from what? From the mass of the people? From unclean things or from unclean people? Be that as it may, the Pharisees formed a special group among the Jews of Palestine, with their own interpretation of the Law of Moses, their own customs and practices, especially on legal points, and their own beliefs on certain matters. They looked on themselves, therefore, as different from all others, and there was in fact a certain cleavage between them and the rest. They also called each other *haver*, literally 'comrade, colleague'. The name is in use today for the members of a collectivist colony (*kibbuz*) in Israel. It is quite likely that the Pharisees were organized in groups called *haveroth* ('unions, clubs'). Josephus says that they were six thousand strong at one time, not counting their wives and children. Most of them probably lived in Jerusalem, as the Gospels indeed suggest.

It is generally assumed that the Pharisees came into existence as a special movement among the pious, the *hasidim* (see above, p. 34). Along with the written Law of Moses, they recognized and upheld an oral tradition, which was also said to derive from Moses, and which, to use their own words, was built as a fence around the Law. Like every other legal system, the Law of Moses cannot do without explanation, jurisprudence and corollary. The lawyer, though often derided, performs a very essential and necessary function in human society. Thus a body of law grew up around the Law of Moses, as its complement, which was passed on by oral and not written tradition. This tradition was not always uniform: opinions and even principles could differ. The Pharisees clung to their own traditions and practices in contrast to others, a contrast which was most marked in the matter of ritual purity. They were so careful that all contact with others was for them a delicate matter. Further, they held that man has an immortal soul that exists after the death of the body. They also believed that his body rises on the last day. They were the most influential party among the people, the chief opponents of Jesus, the party that left its spiritual mark on the people after the fall of the temple. Their successors and spiritual children, the rabbis, committed the oral tradition to writing in the Mishna, the two Talmuds and other books, and made it the official law of Judaism for many centuries.

Beside the Pharisees, and often in opposition to them, stood the Sadducees. According to the most generally accepted view, the name derives from Sadok, the high priest whom Solomon installed after he banished Abiathar, David's favourite, from Jerusalem. Sadok was claimed as ancestor by the high priests and the priests in general who served the second temple, which was built after the exile and destroyed in A.D. 70. The party of the Sadducees was led by the aristocracy of the high-priestly families. The nobility supported it, and above all the well-to-do priests. They did not accept the oral tradition of the Pharisees and they rejected the doctrine of the resurrection, which was a recent arrival among the Jews. Their attitude proves that they were a conservative group which disliked novelties and preferred the practices and the beliefs of the good old days. In the Gospels the Sadducees are often mentioned with the Pharisees as opponents of Jesus.

× Flavius Josephus, Philo and other ancient writers know of another grouping among the Jews of their day, which is not mentioned in the Gospels, namely, the Essenes. The silence of the Gospels is remarkable, and up to now no definitive and satisfactory explanation of it has been found. Other writings, however, are so explicit, and in some cases so circumstantial, that the existence of the Essenes is not matter for doubt.

The name itself is even harder to explain than those of the Pharisees and Sadducees. The Greek texts write it *Essenoi* and *Essaioi*, the latter form being best explained as a transcription of an Aramaic plural *hassaia*, meaning 'trusting' (in God), 'pious'. This explanation tallies with their way of life. Josephus speaks of them more than once in some detail. The Jewish philosopher Philo, a younger contemporary of Jesus, who lived in Alexandria, also mentions them and praises them for their virtuous and exceptional way of life. Even the Roman writer Pliny (died A.D. 79) speaks of them, somewhat sceptically, in a well-known passage as 'a people that lives alone, without women, without lust, without money, in the company of the palms . . . which has persisted for a thousand generations [!] because men tired of life have made their way to it'. They live on the western shore of the Dead Sea, and Engaddi lies to the south of them. This is obviously hearsay, but Pliny records it for what it is worth, without bothering to check the story. The site mentioned is particularly interesting, because it could describe Khirbet Qumran. It is one of the many arguments which have convinced students that Khirbet Qumran was an establishment of the Essenes and that the manuscripts were produced by them. Since these arguments are not of the two-and-two-make-four type, there are still some scholars who do not accept them. But their number is constantly lessening, as the spiritual affinity between the Essenes and the sect of the scrolls becomes ever clearer. To be very cautious, one should say that the connexion is at least highly probable.

The ancient writers tell us that the Essenes practised community of goods, observed celibacy, upheld the Law of Moses strictly, farmed the land, ate in common, were very keen on ritual purity and hence bathed frequently, believed in the immortality of the soul and future bliss, and had other outstanding traits. They were a closed community, which according to Josephus accepted candidates only after a period of probation, first outside and then inside the community. After this trial period, which lasted at least three years, the Essenes had to oblige themselves by a solemn oath to observe the laws of the brotherhood and not to divulge their secrets to outsiders. Alongside this group, the 'strict observants' so to speak, Josephus knew of another whose members were married, but used their marital rights only to beget children. Apart from this their way of life was the same as that of the others. The mention of these 'less rigorous' Essenes indicates the existence of different groups among the Essenes, who can hardly be reduced to merely two types. This observation is important, as it may solve the difficulties that have been urged against the direct identification of the Qumran brotherhood and the Essenes. The latter have indeed been called a 'religious order', and their community building at Qumran has been called a 'monastery', after like institutions in the Catholic Church. Such orders and congregations can look very much alike, especially to outsiders, in spite of minor differences in aim and rule. This may have been also true of the Essenes at one time, though it is not proven.

Along with the Essenes Philo mentions a group, not in Judaea but in Egypt, of men and women whom he calls the 'Therapeuts'. The word had not for him the associations it might have today, and simply meant the 'servants' (of God).

The Essenes represented for Philo the active life, the Therapeuts the contemplative. The Greeks regarded contemplation,
or meditation of the truth, as the highest and noblest activity
of man, and Philo wished to persuade his Greek readers that
anything the heathens did well or nobly, the Jews did too,
and better. He chose as his example of the contemplative life a
group of Jews who lived near Alexandria and there, as he said,
devoted themselves to contemplation. They lived in separate
cells and came out only once a week to hear one of their
number preach on Sacred Scripture, which they then discussed. The other six days were given to prayer and the study
of the Scriptures. Every fiftieth day was a solemn feast-day,
on which they came together for a common meal which was
more like a liturgical ceremony than anything else. They ate
bread with salt and hyssop, drank water and spent the rest of
the time piously. The men and women of the group were all
celibate and had little to do with one another.

Doubts have been cast on the very existence of Philo's
Therapeuts, but wrongly, as seems probable. His picture is
idealized and somewhat tendentious, but if it does not show us
the Therapeuts as they really were, it proves the existence of a
group akin to the Essenes. They too had withdrawn from the
world and led an abstemious life; they too seem to have
observed the fiftieth day with special solemnity.

There are many reasons for identifying the community of
Khirbet Qumran with the Essenes, or at least for putting them
into the category of Essenes. The manuscripts found in Cave 1
include a text which its American editors called 'The Manual
of Discipline', and which is in fact a set of rules for the brotherhood. This rule is represented by no less than eleven fragmentary manuscripts from other caves, which prove that the rule
was not only regularly copied but also worked over and filled
out. There are also fragments of seven manuscripts containing

another set of rules, the ones given by the so-called 'Damascus Document'. This document had been known for many years through medieval copies which had been found at Cairo in 1896 by Rabbi Salomon Schechter of Cambridge, in the lumber-room of a synagogue where worn-out manuscripts were kept, the so-called *genizah*. He published it in 1910. The copies were made in the tenth to twelfth centuries, and may well be connected with the find of manuscripts in A.D. 800, which the Patriarch Timothy relates (see above, p. 23).

But there is no doubt of the close connexion between the Damascus Document and The Manual of Discipline, they display the same characteristics of language, style and vocabulary, and the two sets of rules are closely akin. The differences, which are equally obvious, are explained by attributing the two rules to different stages in the development of the brotherhood; or by assuming that The Manual of Discipline was the rule used at Qumran, while the Damascus Document was for married Essenes; or again, that they cater for groups of different origin, which were, however, closely kindred in spirit. It is better to be sparing of hypotheses as long as all the texts are not published. When taken together at any rate the rules sketch for us a community which coincides with the Essenes in most essentials and in many minor characteristics. We instance: strict community of goods (less strict, or lacking in the Damascus Document); great emphasis on ritual purity and the many ablutions it involved; meals in common; obligatory probation before admittance; the entrance oath; work on the land; belief in an after-life where men join the angels, and so on. The word 'Essenes' must be taken in a broad sense to designate a large group within which differences were possible.

The Essenes go back to the pious Jews of the second century B.C. Their piety was of a special type, though different from

that of the Pharisees. The latter had not isolated themselves
from the people, whereas the Essenes undoubtedly did so.
The finds from the Dead Sea enable us to form a clearer
picture of the Essenes than was hitherto possible. In the next
chapter we shall try to describe the origins and the history of
the Qumran brotherhood, on the basis of our present knowledge.

3

THE QUMRAN BROTHERHOOD AND
ITS PROPHET

THE 'sect' of the Essenes, we saw, sprang from the great
group of pious Jews which lived in Palestine in the
second century before Christ. What this means is best
seen by comparing them with the orthodox Jews of the
twentieth century, who keep the rabbinical law in all its
strictness, even though they live in a country where the
majority of Jews have given it up, and who are known for
their piety and religious practices both by their Jewish and
their non-Jewish neighbours. The *hasidim*, the pious Jews of
Palestine in the time of the second temple, must be regarded
in the same way. They were not a sect, they were not living a
life apart from and totally different from the rest, they did not
even form a party in the beginning. They recognized each
other, they were recognized by others, they easily came
together, being of like mind, and in time of persecution they
closed their ranks, not by founding an organization with
statutes and leadership, but by natural sympathy, just as a
whole people unites when the enemy is in the land.

The pious were therefore on the whole unorganized. But
groups developed among them whose members were more
closely united and so more sharply distinguished from the
outside world. Avoiding for the moment the word 'sect',
which is taken from Josephus and which had a different ring
for him than it has for us, one might speak of a brotherhood.

Such associations for religious purposes were common in the Graeco-Roman world of the day. We remarked in the previous chapter that even ancient Israel had had its groupings; it is not surprising therefore to find similar groups in later times, following perhaps non-Jewish models.

Associations, especially religious brotherhoods, were taken so much for granted in the Graeco-Roman world that little mention is made of them in contemporary literature. They were as popular as they were numerous. At Athens there was a group called the Io-Bacchi, 'servants of the god Bacchus', who came together at certain times to perform their Bacchanalia. By a happy chance the statutes of this association, as it was in the second century A.D., have been preserved. They tell us who could become a member and under what conditions, the days on which they met, how order was to be kept, what penalties were imposed for faults, what was the course of religious ceremonies, how special occasions in the life of the members were to be celebrated, what were the rights and duties of the treasurer, how the members were to show their sympathy at the burial of one of their number. We find modern associations catering for the same interests.

The brotherhood of Qumran was formed along similar lines among the pious Jews of the second century B.C. They were a group of Essenes, *the* Essenes in fact, according to some. We can envisage its formation in two ways: a small number of pious Jews who felt the need of mutual support came together, chose themselves a leader and then developed more widely; or again, perhaps a founder started the group and gathered kindred spirits around him into whom he inculcated his principles. Most probably a group as specialized as the Essenes, or the Qumranites as the case may be, owe their origin to some individual. That would be the most natural process. But there is no express mention of such a founder in the literature that speaks of the Essenes, nor in that of Qumran. Josephus, to be sure, says of the Essenes: 'After God, the name of the lawgiver is greatly venerated by them; whoever blasphemes him is condemned to death.' This is his only mention of such a lawgiver, and the obvious explanation is that he means Moses, who remained always *the* lawgiver in the mind of the Jews. The Qumran rules frequently speak of Moses, and of no one else, as lawgiver. The Damascus Document, however, uses a word from Numbers 21: 18 which can mean both 'staff' and 'chief' and which may also mean 'lawgiver' in this document. If so, it may mean the lawgiver of the brotherhood. We are told that the word is not found in this sense in our Hebrew literature before the fifteenth century.

A number of Qumran texts mention a mysterious personage, whose proper name is never given, called the 'Teacher of righteousness'. He is generally taken to be an historical person, though it has been suggested recently by T. H. Gaster that it is a title whereby all the great teachers of Israel were designated. In the early days of the brotherhood the Teacher was its head and he remained its greatest figure. Since they were under priestly direction, he must himself have been a priest. He came into conflict with the high priest of his day, who is likewise never mentioned by name in the texts now available, but always designated by such expressions as 'the Wicked Priest', 'the Man of Lies', etc.

In one of the Qumran documents, a commentary on Habacuc 1–2 which seeks to apply the prophecy to the writer's day, there is a good deal about Teacher and Priest, which is not always comprehensible. Actual names are nowhere given, and when we come across 'Absalom' we get the impression that the name is a veiled reference to someone unknown. Further, various events are alluded to in a way that is no longer clear to us. The readers of two thousand years ago for whom it was written certainly understood it, but we are mostly at a loss. Scholars have even asked whether the 'Man of Lies' and the 'Wicked Priest' are one and the same person. The texts are in fact so obscure that the question is reasonable. But it seems certain that the expressions which baffle us indicate definite persons, because they occur again and again throughout the Qumran literature.

The picture of the Teacher of righteousness is everywhere the same. He is a priest to whom God gave power to explain the hidden meaning of 'all the words of the prophets'. God raised him up to lead the Israelites in the way of His heart and to make known His judgment upon the ungodly. He has made God's precepts known to Israel. He has at his side a number of kindred spirits who loyally kept the Law. He is opposed by the Wicked Priest who commits a crime against him and his fellows, and persecutes him even in the 'house of his exile' where his enemy appears on the great Day of Expiation to shake his followers' loyalty. That is all we know of him. It is possible but—so far—not proven that the Wicked Priest caused the death of the Teacher. From the texts, we cannot be certain. The Habacuc Commentary speaks only in general terms of a conflict between the Teacher and the Priest. We cannot make out the course of events.

It may be that we do know more about the Teacher. For not only was he written about, he may possibly have written about himself. A number of hymns, hitherto unknown, were found in the first cave, and the speaker in several of these hymns is held by many to be the Teacher himself. Following David, the great singer of Israel's psalms, poets were never lacking in Israel and they practised their art down to the last epoch of the Old Testament. The author of the first book of Maccabees grows constantly lyrical when telling the deeds of his heroes and expresses himself in poetical form. Jesus ben Sirach, the author of Ecclesiasticus, who wrote about 190 B.C., closed his book of aphorisms with a long psalm of thanksgiving, after having often become lyrical. The brotherhood of Qumran too had its singers, and it is noteworthy that many of their psalms begin with the words 'I will praise Thee', like the psalm at the end of Ecclesiasticus, with which they often agree in style. They were written in the contemporary mode, at least in part. To some extent they consist of quotations from or reminiscences of the Old Testament, which came spontaneously to the lips of the authors. But the Thanksgiving Psalms also contain elements wholly their own.

These hymns often introduce a speaker who has a very special standing among his friends and fellows. There is nothing very special about his constant complaint of persecution on the part of wicked men who seek his life: that is a theme which occurs in a large number of Old Testament psalms, and in the psalm of Ecclesiasticus. But it is significant that the author complains of 'being driven from his land, like a bird from its nest' (Hymns 4: 8). The form of the verb (imperfect, which here stands for the present tense) could indicate that the author is still exiled from his land or home. Through him God has 'illuminated the face of many, and strengthened them to be a great multitude'; God has constantly 'made known to him His wonderful secrets', and done wonderful and mighty works through him in the sight of many. God has poured out His holy spirit upon him so that he does not stumble, but is full of joy. God has established him as a lofty sign (text: standard) for the justified and the elect, as one who, knowing wonderful secrets, can give wise counsel. God has put the right words on his lips and taught him wisdom. He has made his heart a fountain of wisdom which he shares with all who understand; but to the dull he speaks a different

language, to make their guilt evident. God has made him 'a
father to those who are the object of [God's] love', a protector
to those who are a sign (for others). He attributes his miseries
ultimately to the sins he has committed.

Not all the traits of this portrait are strictly individual.
The sage of Ecclesiasticus also wishes to impart his wisdom to
a great number; in fact, he wishes to pour forth his doctrine like
prophecy, and to leave it to posterity after him (Ecclesiasticus 24:
33 [46]), which is one way of saying that he is inspired. But there
are many places in the Hymns where one cannot but feel that a
leader of a group is speaking. The inference is all the more easy
because one knows that there was such a leader, the Teacher
of righteousness, and hence the data may be said to complete
one another. Be that as it may, there is much to say for
identifying the author of some at least of the newly-found
psalms with the Teacher of righteousness, though we cannot
simply say that the identification is to be regarded as established.

So the picture of the Teacher given us in the Damascus
Document and in various commentaries may be completed by
traits taken from the psalms. The Teacher appears in a very
special light as one who is convinced that he is inspired by
God, initiated into divine secrets and enlightened by God with
regard to the hidden meaning of the prophets' words. These
'secrets' are not precisely what we call the wholly supernatural
mysteries of the divine nature, which surpass human understanding, but mostly the mysterious plans of God's providence
and in particular, the divine decrees concerning the salvation
and the judgment of mankind, which God had long kept
secret but finally revealed to the Teacher. The mysteries are
conceived of as the decisions of a ruler, which are first taken
in privy council and only later promulgated. The Teacher has
gathered a group of disciples around him which has grown

very numerous; he has made known to them all the revelations which he was granted, but above all he has taught them to observe strictly the Law of Moses. All who keep the Law and are loyal to the Teacher have nothing to fear from God's judgment. His opponents, led by a 'Wicked Priest' make things so difficult for the good priest that he is forced to leave his country, or at least his home. But he is not left in peace even in 'exile'. Finally some grave injustice is done him: what precisely, we do not know.

As to the identity of this Teacher of righteousness, we are so far completely in the dark. Several names have been put forward, e.g. Onias III, the Jewish high priest who was murdered at Daphne near Antioch in 171 B.C. But they are all guesses. So far the Essenes have succeeded admirably in keeping the name of their Teacher a secret. It cannot be proved that he was their founder, but he must have been their great prophet and organizer.

When even the name of the Teacher is unknown, it is difficult to ascribe to him a date. Efforts have been made to fix it by determining the identity of his adversary, the 'Wicked Priest'. Everything points to the latter's being a high priest, and since the brotherhood was founded in the second or first century B.C., history provides a whole row of names to choose from. It looks as if scholars have gone the round of them, because there is not one of them that has not been put forward by one scholar or another as candidate for the role of 'Wicked Priest'. Who can it have been? One of the high priests of the time of Antiochus Epiphanes who was hand in glove with this heathen king? Jonathan Simon (161–143 B.C.)? John Hyrcan (135–104 B.C.)? Aristobulus I (104–103 B.C.)? Alexander Jannaeus (103–76 B.C.)? Aristobulus II (67–63 B.C.)? Hyrcan II (76–67 B.C. and 63–40 B.C.)? Antigonus (40–37 B.C.)? These names exhaust the possibilities, because the upper limit seems to be fixed by the persecutions under Antiochus Epiphanes, while the lower limit is the beginning of the reign of Herod the Great. The Wicked Priest had undoubtedly great powers and apparently could do what he liked in the country. Hence he cannot be placed in the time of Herod or later.

Pg 39
'RAGING
LION

The present writer had for some time past considered Alexander Jannaeus as a serious candidate; and with the publication in June 1956 of a chance fragment of a commentary on Nahum, this view has become a certainty in the eyes of several scholars. The commentary is of the same type as that on Habacuc: the prophet's words are seen and explained in the perspective of the writer's day. Like the other commentaries, it speaks of a conflict; but unlike the others, it mentions names, undoubtedly those of Syrian kings. It speaks of a '[Deme]trius, king of Greece [=Hellenized Syria], who tried to enter Jerusalem by the counsel of the seekers after smooth things.' Now Syria had three kings called Demetrius: Demetrius I (162–150 B.C.); II (145–126 B.C.); III (some time between 95 and 83 B.C.). The last was one of five brothers who disputed each other's claim to the kingdom of their father Antiochus VIII after his death, and waged war to seize as much as possible of their paternal heritage. Demetrius III Eucaerus saw a chance of making himself master of Damascus and some of the surrounding territory, but while fighting his brother Philip in the north of the country in 88 or 87 B.C. he was taken prisoner by his brother and died in captivity. This is the Demetrius who was called in by the Pharisees in their struggle against Alexander Jannaeus, as we saw in the previous chapter. He invaded Palestine, in the hope of extending his territory, but went no farther than Sichem. He retired after winning a battle, when six thousand Jews who had been on his side went over to Alexander.

We know that Demetrius I sent several generals to Judaea

to attack Judas Maccabaeus, at a time when Jerusalem was still
in the power of the king. It cannot therefore be so easily said
of him that 'he tried to enter Jerusalem', while it may well be
supposed that Demetrius III had this object in view, because it
was the capital city of his adversary, Alexander. Demetrius II
seems to be out of the question. Hence a number of scholars
think it probable that the author of the Nahum Commentary
meant the third king of that name when he spoke of Demetrius. If so, he cannot have written before 88 B.C.

An incomplete line of the text contains the words: 'the
kings of Greece [Syria], till the rise of the rulers of the Kittim'.
With the Greeks thus contrasted with the Kittim, these last
can hardly be any but the Romans, as in Daniel 11: 30 and,
as many hold, in the Habacuc Commentary. If so, our text
must refer to the coming of the Romans to the Near East,
especially Syria. This took place in stages and the Romans only
really interested themselves in Syria when Pompey led his
armies in triumph through the Near East and took Jerusalem
in 63 B.C.

The commentary also speaks of a 'Raging Lion' (literally,
the Lion of Wrath), a personage known to the author and
regarded by him as the 'ravening lion' of Nahum 2: 13. With
his lords and counsellors, he did much evil; one of his crimes
was to hang men alive on the gibbet. Antiochus Epiphanes
had put Jews to death by crucifixion, but the first Jewish ruler
who is known to have done so is Alexander Jannaeus, the
adversary of the Demetrius whose name occurs a little earlier
in the commentary. The question arises whether Alexander
is not the 'Raging Lion'. We may go a step further and ask
ourselves whether the 'Raging Lion' is not the same as the
'Wicked Priest', the 'Man of Lies', of the Habacuc Commentary. The latter occurs at any rate in different commentaries
(Habacuc, Micheas, Psalm 37, i.e. in three out of four

commentaries of any size yet published), which suggests that he was *the* great enemy of Qumran. Hence the identification of the Wicked Priest, the opponent of the Teacher, with Alexander Jannaeus has much to be said for it, though it is not yet fully proven. The Teacher would have lived about the same time, in the first quarter of the first century B.C., and the brotherhood will have been founded then, or at least given its definitive form by the Teacher's revelations.

The excavations that have been going on at Khirbet Qumran and the environs every year since November–December 1951 throw some more light on the story. The Khirbet (ruins) is about eight miles south of Jericho and half a mile inland from the western shore of the Dead Sea, on a stony marl terrace which runs north–south between the level ground by the shore and the steep rocky cliffs of the foothills of the Judaean desert. A thousand yards north-west of the Khirbet lies the famous cave in the cliffs where the first finds of manuscripts were made. Two miles to the south lies the spring, Ain Feshkha, after which the manuscripts were first named, because no one then associated Khirbet Qumran with the cave. The meaning of the word Qumran is still unknown. One author solved the riddle by deriving it from the word *qamar*, 'moon', on the romantic plea that the inmates of the building prayed by moonlight. It is true that vigils were held at Qumran, but there is no text that associates these nocturnal devotions with the moon. The Palestine moon may be brighter than ours, but no one could have read Hebrew texts for long by its light.

The ruins, which formed originally a rectangle of some thirty by forty yards, had been known for a long time. Several explorers had described them, the first over a hundred years ago. In the light of the knowledge then available, they seemed to be the remains of a Roman fort. Now there are so

many Roman remains in the Near East that special reasons
would have been needed to launch an investigation of these
particular ruins, since there were so many older and more
interesting things to explore. Hence the ruins of Qumran
were ignored. Only the most detailed maps indicated them,
and only a rare scholar gave them a short mention.

When the famous first cave was found, and fragments of
manuscripts turned up elsewhere, R. de Vaux, o.p., and G. L.
Harding decided to see whether the Khirbet had anything to
do with them. The results far surpassed expectations and not
one but six campaigns of excavation were undertaken in the
following years. During several weeks' work each year, the
Khirbet was fully investigated and the remains of the buildings
laid bare. It was clearly not a Roman fort, though it had been
used as such for some years; on the contrary, it was closely
associated with the caves, the manuscripts, and the users of the
manuscripts. Further, it was possible to determine pretty
accurately the periods at which the building was put up,
damaged, abandoned, rebuilt and reoccupied and finally
abandoned.

At present it is easy to reach Khirbet Qumran. If one does
not belong to the staff of scholars which goes there regularly
one must have a letter of recommendation, likewise a safe-
conduct, which the Rockefeller Museum provides under
certain conditions. Then one hires a taxi, which is not too
expensive for a group of four or six, and sets out over the
hairpin bends of the winding road to Jericho. An early morning start is best. The Jericho road was laid down under the
British Mandate, and runs at some distance from the old
Roman road which dates from the time of Jesus. A twenty
miles' run, during which the road drops three thousand feet,
brings one to the plain of Jericho. Here it is much warmer
than in Jerusalem and in the summer almost unbearably so.

Herod had his winter palace there, and the late King Abdullah of Jordan, who was assassinated, used to go there each winter for the soft warm air. Before reaching Jericho, one turns right and then right again. The road is now passable enough at first, and takes one to a police post where one shows one's documents and exchanges a few words with the policemen, if one can speak Arabic. Shortly after that, the road becomes no more than a track, a sort of trail marked out by one's forerunners in this part of the country. The track takes one uphill and downhill, past places where the water has made its way to the Dead Sea, cutting out gullies in the ground, and leaving behind it pebbles and stones. If it is raining, the car will go no further, not even if it is a jeep. If it is dry, the car can go on, but only with difficulty, and at times it will seem that it can't be done. When Khirbet Qumran comes in sight at last, after a long and difficult pull, the driver gives up, protests that he can go no further and has in fact already gone too far, and points out the rest of the way, which is to be done on foot. A few minutes' march brings one, if one climbs the plateau at the right place, to a mass of ruins of grey stone, not very tall, which at first sight show very little shape and no beauty at all. This is Khirbet Qumran, very probably the headquarters of the brotherhood which is mostly identified with the Essenes.

There is a central building, with annexes. The main block is some forty yards long and from twenty to thirty yards wide. The tallest portion of the remains is in the north-west corner, somewhat detached from the rest. It is a tower, thirty-five by forty feet at the base, with massive walls nearly five feet thick. The tower was built for defence, no exaggerated precaution in the wild desert by the Dead Sea. A courtyard on which a number of rooms opened formed the rest of the main block. In the south-east corner there was a large reservoir, cut out of the rock, the bottom of which is reached by a flight of steps over eighteen feet long. The steps are now split all along their length, as the result of an earthquake which left one side of them a foot and a half lower than the other. The walls of the cistern are still covered to a great extent by the plaster that was used on the inside to make it watertight. To the east of this cistern lie a number of shallow basins which are so close to each other that archaeologists see in them a primitive wash-room (laundry?). Then there are the remains of ovens, a room with a low bench along the walls, the remains of a small colonnade, etc. Outside this central block one can observe, especially on the south and west sides, a number of cisterns, the remains of workrooms, including a pottery-works, a water-main which linked up with the hills and provided the whole system of cisterns with water, and the outline of a great hall. Its walls still rise a few feet above the ground, and the stone bases of three pillars which held up the roof at the east end are still visible. On the west side of this hall is a small room containing large quantities of earthenware, bowls, platters, etc., the tableware of the community.

The visitors may not see or recognize all of this, because the excavators have not left everything in its place, and have removed a number of objects. One must be prepared for this when one visits excavation-sites in the East, so it is best to study plans and descriptions of them beforehand, and if possible to tour them with an expert, map in hand.

Jars of exactly the same shape as those in which the first scrolls were found have turned up in the remains of this building, and they correspond also to the careful reconstructions which the experts performed on the pottery fragments from the caves. It follows that the building and the caves belong together, and likewise that the jars were not made specially for the manuscripts but were for household use.

A building such as that of Qumran cannot have been the

dwelling-house of private individuals. It clearly belonged to a community and was destined for community use. Many rooms were obviously for the storage of provisions and the like; others were halls where a large number of people could meet. The many cisterns, now numbered at thirteen, must have served the needs of large numbers. The cisterns were fed from above by a channel which was partly cut in the rock, partly made of cement. There are no wells higher up, but when heavy rain falls in the winter on the plateau above the rocky slope, the water flows to the lower levels, as the rocky ground above does not absorb it. It flows down through wadis, or is held in all sorts of natural reservoirs, from which the ancient inhabitants of the community building led it to their cisterns.

How is the building to be dated? The archaeologists had not much difficulty, because they found enough pottery and above all, enough coins to help them to solve the question. Many of the coins were so corroded that they could not be identified at once, hence lists were not published immediately. A report which appeared in 1954 gave the following: three silver coins of Antiochus VII, from 136, 130 and 129 B.C.; fourteen of John Hyrcan (135–104 B.C.); thirty-eight of Alexander Jannaeus (103–76 B.C.); fifteen of Hasmonaean rulers who were more definitely fixed; two of Antigonus Mathathias (40–37 B.C.); one silver coin of Tyre (29 B.C.); six of Archelaus (4 B.C.–A.D. 6); thirty from the time of the Roman governors under Augustus, Tiberius, Claudius and Nero (A.D. 6–67); eleven from the second year of the first revolt (A.D. 67–68); a couple from the years A.D. 67–73; three from A.D. 79; one from A.D. 86; thirteen from the time of the second revolt (A.D. 132–135) and five from Byzantine and Arab times, three of which were found on the surface. From 1954 to 1956 many more coins were added to the collection, and from

the report published in 1956, it is clear that they come from
the same general period as the others. An out-of-the-way
discovery was made at the beginning of 1955. Under the floor
of a small room in one of the annexes three jars were found
which contained over 550 silver pieces, nearly all Tyrian, of
the first century B.C. and none later than 9–8 B.C. This treasure
—for that is what it was—was hidden in an unusual place: why,
and by whom, remains an enigma. One of the three jars is now
on exhibition in the Palestine Museum at Jerusalem; it lies on
its side in a glass case, and the coins, brightly polished, seem to
be pouring from the jar as though from a cornucopia. With
regard to the history of the building, the jar only tells us that
it was in existence when the treasure was buried there. If the
treasure had no long history behind it when it came to rest
here, we can say that it was buried not long after 9–8 B.C., that
is, towards the end of the reign of Herod.

The coins that have been found in various parts of the
building are luckily so numerous and so diverse that they can
be used to determine with great probability the various phases
of the history of the building. But one must be cautious,
because a coin can have been still in use a long time after it
was struck, so that its date does not necessarily indicate the
epoch in which it happened to come to rest. Coins of Queen
Victoria were still circulating before the last war in England,
but they were scarce compared with those of George V and
VI. If a number of coins are found together, of which the great
majority come from a certain period, one can generally say
that they were deposited during that period or not long after.

The first type of coin found in any great number at Qumran
dates from the time of Alexander Jannaeus. There are indeed
enough from the time of John Hyrcan to make it impossible
to exclude the existence of the building in his reign, but clearly
its first great days were under Jannaeus, and if it had been

built before his reign, it had not long existed when he came
to the throne. Practically no coins of the reign of Herod have
been found, if one excepts the buried treasure mentioned
above, which still remains a mystery. The building must have
been abandoned under Herod, but it was reoccupied during
the time of the Roman procurators. Some decades after the
destruction of Jerusalem (A.D. 70) it was again empty. It was
occupied again during the second revolt (132–135), after
which it was abandoned for good. Long afterwards, a few
men used the ruins at odd times. They lost a few coins there
that they never found again, and which are now museum
pieces.

The ruins themselves offer an explanation of the remarkable
fact that they were not occupied during the reign of Herod.
Traces of a crack in the walls and floors are clearly visible in
many places; the steps leading down to one of the cisterns are
split down the middle, so badly that one side is a foot and a
half lower than the other. Fractures have been observed in the
masonry of the great tower and elsewhere. The obvious
explanation is an earthquake, a common phenomenon in this
region, and in Palestine and Syria in general, even to quite
recently. The latest to be reported affected the Lebanese city
of Beirut and a region to the south of it. It took place in the
early part of 1956 and the resulting devastation was a national
catastrophe for Lebanon. Now, we know that a severe earthquake shook Judaea in 31 B.C. According to Josephus it caused
the deaths of 30,000 men, to say nothing of the cattle. This
number is certainly much too high, but it tells us something
of the impression made by the catastrophe. Herod was at war
at the time, and had just arrived with his army at the plain of
Jericho, not far from the Jordan. Panic threatened to get the
better of his troops, but he succeeded in calming them and
marching them over the Jordan.

After the destruction caused by the earthquake, the owners apparently did not rebuild the community houses for a long time. We can only guess at their reasons. It has been suggested that Herod had something to do with it. The king had a magnificent winter palace at Jericho, and his way of life certainly did not come up to the ideals of the Essenes of Qumran, to put it mildly. Herod could play the Jew when among the Jews, but he was a heathen among the heathen, cruel with the cruel and evil with the evil. Possibly the Essenes reproached him for his conduct, just as later on John the Baptist was to reproach another Herod. It may be that the first Herod used the opportunity offered by the earthquake to bar the Essenes from their centre at Qumran. They returned there after his death.

On the basis of these and some other data, we can give the following outline of the history of the building.

For some reason as yet unknown, a pious group of the Essene type betook themselves to the shore of the Dead Sea and looked for a suitable spot to settle in. They chose a site which had been already inhabited in the time of the kings of Judah, and hence offered possibilities for human settlement. The climate is pleasant in winter, but so sultry in the summer that even modern archaeologists cannot bear it for long. But they have to work in the summer whereas the early inhabitants could relax during the great heats. Cultivation was possible around the well of Ain Feshkha three thousand yards away, and perhaps at other places on the hills near by. Further, it was possible to study and meditate there undisturbed. They read the Law and the prophets and other pious books, as we read in the great Rule: 'And when all this comes to pass with the community, in Israel, according to this rule, they must separate themselves from the dwelling-places of sinners to go out to the desert, to prepare the way before HIM [God], as is written: Prepare in the desert a way for Yahweh, make straight in the wilderness a path for our God' (Manual 8: 12–14). The text invoked is from Isaiah 40:3. It played an important role in the preaching of John the Baptist, about whom the question is often asked, was he an Essene? Was the text itself the reason for their withdrawal to the desert? This is not certain, because the words were interpreted allegorically: 'The desert is the study of the Law which [God] has laid down through Moses' (Manual 8: 15). But the two things probably went together. They moved out to the desert, to an inhospitable spot, in order to study the Law and the prophets.

Could not the Law be studied everywhere? Certainly it could, and the many scribes of Jesus' time did so. Philo says that the Essenes avoided cities on account of the corrupt morals of such places. They lived, he says, 'in villages' (literally, in village fashion). This must mean that they lived not inside but outside the walls of the towns, or in little villages in the country. More easily than in a town, they could find there a place where they could live in community and keep themselves ritually pure as far as possible. In Palestine there is, and there was, no essential difference between city and village. For reasons of security, no one lived alone in the country, as is still to some extent true today; in a given region, the inhabitants all came together in one place. If such a spot was walled in ancient times, it could be called a city in Greek; if it was open, a village. The lack of any essential difference between city and village makes it possible for Josephus to say that the Essenes had no 'city' of their own, but that there were colonies of them in various 'cities'. Obviously, he does not distinguish between city and village, and so does not necessarily contradict Philo.

We cannot exclude the possibility that the Essenes, or a group of them, withdrew to the desert because people were making their life too difficult where they were living. In a hymn which many take to have been composed by the great Teacher of the group, the author complains that 'he is driven from his land like a bird from the nest'. The Habacuc Commentary says that the Wicked Priest did not leave the Teacher of righteousness in peace even 'in the house of his exile'. Once they had fled perforce to the desert, they could see in it afterwards a disposition of divine providence and then find this in the Bible. So far we have no more than suspicions and guesses. We really do not know.

The group settled down in the desert of Judah in a place which had been inhabited four or five centuries earlier. When they arrived the place was probably deserted and abandoned, and they began by putting up a great community building of which the outer walls formed what was almost a rectangle, forty yards long and twenty-five to thirty yards broad. The walls were of roughly dressed stones, in between which were fillings of a mortar made of earth. The walls were mostly about two feet four inches thick. They built a staunch tower in the north-west corner, with walls from four to six feet thick. There was a courtyard in the middle, on to which opened various rooms, on two storeys. Undoubtedly, the tower was for defence; store-rooms were provided on the ground-floor, and there were three rooms which served other purposes on the upper level. A winding staircase in the south-west corner of the tower led from one floor to the other. Two cisterns were installed in the east wing of the building, and a number of small basins, each lower than the next, which makes the archaeologists think of a laundry. The insides of the cisterns were plastered, as were also the inside walls of the building. There were also workshops, and a latrine. Wood was used in the building, while the roofs were, at least in part, made of reeds, as may still be seen in many houses in the

Arab city of Jericho. Particular attention was bestowed on the water-supply.

It is very probable that the Teacher of righteousness lived in this building, as did his followers; it is certainly possible that he was responsible for its construction, though we cannot say more. There is no doubt whatever that the house was a centre, round which a settlement was grouped, and round which, in the environs, men lived in caves or in tents. Of this last assertion we have proof in the tent-pegs and the remains of utensils that have been found in the neighbouring caves. It is noteworthy that coins have been found so far only in the main building, and nowhere else. The best explanation of this seems to be given by the ideals of the inmates, who had no personal, but only community property. Thus the texts explain the archaeological findings, and the findings confirm the texts.

Nothing like a common dormitory has yet been found, but it is not really missing. Palestine contains the remains of many Christian monasteries of the Byzantine era, and dormitories have been found in very few of them. Anyone with personal experience of the East will not find this strange; the simple folk need very little sleeping facilities, nothing more than a mat, a cloak, some sort of covering, because they can always find a place to unroll a mat and stretch out.

When a member of the community died, he was buried in the fields outside the main building, in a simple but remarkable fashion. His brethren made a groove running from north to south, with a hollow at the bottom on one side to hold the corpse, which was buried without any adornment, possibly even without any clothing. No funeral gifts were placed along with the dead. When in place, the corpse was covered with a layer of stones, after which the grave was filled with earth. On top of the grave another layer of stones was placed, in the form of an oval, and the burial was complete. No names of the dead have been found, and no indication of rank or identity. The dead man lay on his back, the hands crossed at the waist or stretched out by the side, the head mostly pointing south.

It has been estimated that there are about eleven hundred graves in the burial-ground east of Qumran. Only a small number of them have been investigated, because the difference between one and another of them does not seem significant. They are not all quite alike; the recess for the corpse, which in most graves is along the east side, is along the west in some cases, and missing altogether in others. Sometimes the head of the corpse is towards the north, while some graves run from east to west. Only one of the dead was buried in a wooden coffin. Most of the skeletons examined so far are those of males, but there are some skeletons of women and children.

What the cemetery and the manner of burial signify may be seen from the writings of the group. These show us that the members of the brotherhood were convinced that they would be received into the company of the angels after their death. They had ceased to think of a sojourn in the darkness of the underworld, at least for the pious members of the brotherhood. Heathens, and the Israelites in earlier times, were accustomed to provide the dead with food for their journey to the underworld; they poured water on the graves to provide them with refreshment. They added ornaments, and even weapons for the men, to be used in the hereafter if possible. None of this is found among the Essenes. When they laid their dead naked in the ground, they may have been thinking explicitly of the words of Job: 'Naked I came from my mother's womb, naked do I return' (Job 1: 21). The depth of the graves—four to six feet—and the careful covering of the corpse with stones, after it was laid in a recess in the stony ground, may have been an effort to protect the bones as well as possible, with a view to the resurrection. It may, however, have been simply a pious precaution to guard the dead against the jackals and hyenas which one can see from Qumran every day and hear every night.

An enigma as yet unsolved is the fact that remains of beasts were also interred with care. This had already been published in learned periodicals when Father de Vaux, at the Second Old Testament Congress in Strasburg, August 1956, reported that forty to forty-five of such burials had been found in open spaces round the building. Most of them belonged to its first period, but a number belonged to the second, and by no means all have been dug up. There are bones of sheep, goats, cows, calves and lambs, that is, beasts of which the flesh was eaten, and which could also be offered in the temple. They are the remains of meals, because the bones are often from more than one beast and the skeletons are not complete. They were buried after being picked clean, and some of them show traces of fire, presumably from roasting. They were buried in jars or covered with large potsherds.

Meat is a luxury food in the East, which the people of the desert eat only a few days in the year, making quite an occasion of it. The Essenes, whose austerity was so highly esteemed by ancient writers, cannot have eaten it every day. The bones must be the remains of very occasional meals. Had these meals a religious character? Were they perhaps Paschal meals? Most probably not, because the remains of the Paschal lamb had to be burnt (Exodus 12: 10). Did the Essenes, in their exaggerated fear of uncleanness, perhaps regard animal bones as also unclean, and bury them carefully in such a way as to exclude all further contact with them? Were they buried in jars to prevent the jackals from digging them up? Were they preserved as well as possible because the Essenes attached some particular significance to the bones? This last solution has little to recommend it, but no satisfactory answer can be given to any of the above questions, if one is shy of pure guess-work. We have here one of the enigmas of Qumran, and we can only hope that new finds, or the decipherment of texts, may cast some light on the question. Scholars have so far noted one parallel: the bones left over from animal sacrifices of Punic origin. These have been found in sanctuaries in North Africa and Sardinia, buried in urns or dishes and surmounted by sacred pillars.

The brotherhood of Qumran lived in and around the building for more than three quarters of a century. We are as yet ignorant of their history during that period. The Teacher of righteousness may have lived there for many years. Possibly he received there the hostile visit of the Jerusalem high priest, of which the Habacuc Commentary speaks. If so the halls of Qumran rang to a dramatic conflict, when the teacher of the group was opposed by the supreme authority of the nation. The high priest hardly came alone. Did he have the Teacher arrested? Did he mishandle him? Or did he have him killed? These questions must also remain unanswered for the present, unless one is content with guesses.

A crude construction like that of Qumran must have needed constant repairs during the long years of the first period of its existence, and perhaps new rooms were added. It was no longer new when in 31 B.C. it suffered a terrible disaster: the earthquake which caused widespread devastation in Judaea and of which we have spoken above. The shock was so severe that apparently even the massive walls of the tower were unable to withstand it; the tower split, the stone lintel over a door broke in two, the roofs collapsed. The heaviest damage was done in the east wing of the building where, for instance, the rock-cut steps leading down into a cistern split so sharply down the middle that one half settled a foot and a half lower than the other. It is not surprising that after such a tremor the walls fell in and the whole structure of the building was damaged. It became totally uninhabitable in a few minutes, and the first period of its history was closed.

After the earthquake, the building was abandoned for a time. When one looks for reasons, the questions begin to pile up again. Did Herod the Great dislike the Essenes' way of life so much that he prevented their resuming it so near his winter palace? Was the building so badly damaged that they lacked the means of restoring it, or did they lose courage at the extent of the damage? Had the brotherhood established itself so comfortably elsewhere that they no longer felt the need of a settlement, or headquarters, in so remote a part of the desert? These questions cannot yet be answered, but the last is worth discussing.

We have already had occasion to mention the so-called 'Damascus Document'. According to C. Rabin, a Jewish scholar who re-edited it recently, this text is composed of two different documents, one an admonition, the other a series of laws, both part of the Qumran writings, as is proved by the language and the style, and by the fact that they are represented among the fragments from the caves. The document has been known by various names. Its first editor called it a 'Zadokite Work', i.e. a work produced by the 'sons' or followers of a certain Zadok (Sadoq). Its authors have also been known as the 'Covenanters of Damascus' and the work itself as the 'Damascus Document' because it speaks of 'a new covenant in the land of Damascus', where priests, levites and pious people from the land of Judah had betaken themselves, as the document says, or seems to say: 'The well is the Law, and they that digged it are they . . . who left the land of Judah

1. Road running north from Ain Feshkha. The ruins of Khirbet Qumran are at the extreme right of the plateau seen in the centre of the picture.

2. Ain Feshkha (the spring of Feshkha) at the foot of the hills of the Judean Desert. Khirbet Qumran is two and a half miles to the north. The Dead Sea is in the background.

3. Cave One, where the largest and most important manuscripts were found in 1947. Bottom left : two entrances made by the investigators. Above the one to the right is the small, original opening.

4. Site of the famous Cave Four, east of Khirbet Qumran. The holes in the middle were made by the investigators, to clear out the rubble which is seen at the bottom. The original opening is on top, towards the back.

5. Khirbet Mird. Explored by the Belgian expedition under Professor de Langhe.

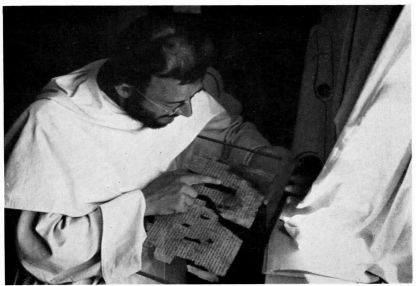

6. Fr. Barthélemy examining the Two-Column Document, annexed to the Manual of Discipline.

7. Mar Athanasius Jesus Samuel, Bishop of St. Mark's Monastery, Jerusalem ; purchaser of scrolls from Cave One. Photograph taken in July 1947.

and sojourned in the land of Damascus' (Damascus Document 6: 5). The text seems clear enough, but many scholars think otherwise, and not without reason. Some think that the land of Damascus is nothing else but the region of Qumran, either because 'Damascus' is simply a symbolic name, such as occurs elsewhere in the Qumran writings, or because the region could be reckoned as part of a territory of which Damascus was the chief city. Others hold that the 'exile in Damascus' is a reminiscence of the text of Amos: 'I will cause you to go into captivity beyond Damascus' (Amos 5: 27) and refers to the exile of the whole people, which took place centuries before, and not to the exile of the brotherhood.

Thus the apparently firm hypothesis, that the inmates of Qumran emigrated to Damascus after the earthquake, turns out to be quite shaky. All the more so, because we cannot be quite certain that the Damascus Document, or at least the legal part of it, comes from exactly the same group as lived at Qumran; it may come from another branch of the movement. There are at any rate marked differences between these laws and The Manual of Discipline. These are sometimes explained by saying that the two sets of laws represent different stages of the development of the group. On the whole, the Manual is looked on as the older, but there are reasons also for thinking it the later document, for instance, because it insists on community of goods much more strictly than the Damascus Document.

Whatever happened, it was thirty years before the same group of men that had lived there previously returned to Qumran. The building was restored to its former condition; the breaches in the damaged defensive tower were made good, and it was shored up by a strong stone rampart which was built all round the base. This new wall was thirteen feet high and from four to six feet thick. Some small changes were made in the building itself: a door or gate was bricked up, another was opened up, a small room opening on the inner yard was built on, etc. The two inside cisterns were so badly damaged that they were left as they were; a wall was thrown up to the west of them, and it looks as if the whole south-east corner (cisterns, wash-house, etc.) was left an open courtyard. To the south of the building a large new reservoir was cut in the rock. Other cisterns were added outside, and on the east a long wall was built which ran practically north–south and made an acute angle with the old eastern outer wall.

In this second period the annexes, which had already been discovered during the excavations of 1954, were extended and improved. The whole structure reminds one strongly of a modern or medieval monastery (there is no great difference). The community possessed a complete pottery-works, various ovens for baking bread, others perhaps for smelting metal, threshing-floors, a kitchen, a large refectory, etc. The kitchen opened directly on the refectory, and in it the remains of no less than a thousand pieces of crockery were found, including some seven hundred round bowls. When one remembers the importance which orthodox Jews still attach to the ritual 'cleanness' of the dishes they eat from, this find is not surprising. It may also be that some of this pottery was to be sold, but a large community needed a great number of bowls and plates if it was determined to preserve its 'purity' always intact. There was also a milling-plant for grinding corn. Thus the community was self-supporting, and since there must have been some things that they had to buy, the production of utensils was probably to help their income. We know that the Christian monks of Egypt and Palestine supported themselves by weaving baskets, which they themselves sold in the market.

Writing also went on in the building. When some remarkable pieces of tile and plaster were found in the ruins, it was thought at first that they were the remains of a ceiling. But when they had been painstakingly assembled, like a jig-saw puzzle, they turned out to be the remains of writing-desks. Two ink-wells of a standard pattern, one of bronze, the other of earthenware, were found near by. One of the tables is sixteen feet long, though only a foot and a half high; a couple of others are shorter. They appear to have run along the walls of an upper room which fell in at the second destruc-tion of the building. A writing-desk only a foot and a half high seems somewhat low, and so it would be for us, but the Oriental of the old school does not sit on a chair but cross-legged on the ground. The position is very tiring for one who is not used to it, but quite comfortable if it has been practised from early youth. That is the way Jesus was sitting, no doubt, when the scribes and Pharisees brought him a woman taken in adultery, and he wrote with his finger on the ground while they were accusing her. In the writing-room, as on the ground-floor, there was a low step running along the base of the walls. Probably the mats on which they sat were unrolled on this step. What kind of writing they were engaged upon is clear enough from the many remains of book-rolls in the caves.

Thus in the second period of the building, life went on as during the first. Though the house was a community building, it was too small for the brotherhood. Many lived in tents and caves. Were the tent-dwellers perhaps visitors, seeking edification at the headquarters of the brotherhood? Or were the tents used when it was too hot to stay in the building? Do they perhaps explain the fact that some of the brotherhood was said at times to be 'in camps'? Many towns-folk of the Near East build themselves huts of leaves and branches outside or on top of their houses during the hot season, and use them for sleeping in. No doubt the same custom was practised at Qumran.

On one point we have still no information: how and where the brethren held their religious services. We know that the Essenes refused to take part in the temple cult at Jerusalem, probably because they held it was not ritually pure, and also because they disapproved of the conduct of the priests. The community of Qumran dreamed of the day when its own priests could direct a purified and renovated form of the sacrificial liturgy. But that day was still to come, and if Qumran did not invent its own rites (and it is most improbable that they did) their religious reunions must have been very like the synagogue services. No special building was needed for the purpose, and they may have used their great hall, which was perhaps also their refectory, or one of the larger rooms, for their services.

The second period of the community building lasted a little shorter than the first. It has been suggested that John the Baptist grew up there during this period. After all, did he not go to the desert as a child? Why did he preach and baptize at the Jordan? Why do the Gospels link his preaching with the text of Isaiah 40: 3 f., 'The voice of one crying in the wilderness, make straight the path of the Lord', a text which the community of Qumran applied to itself, as we have seen above. Undoubtedly, the Baptist reminds us in many ways of the views, the way of life and the practices of the Essenes. But to call him an Essene, and to assert that he grew up at Qumran, is going beyond the evidence. We know far too little as yet about the diverse forms of piety which flourished among the Jews of Jesus' time. Others may have been inspired by the Essenes to take up a way of life which in some ways resembled theirs, and Essenism may have been a movement with many facets, embracing various groups, and there may have been other groups besides. The Baptist may have belonged to one of these.

When *The Illustrated London News* (3 September 1955) published a set of photographs of Qumran, it went so far as to suggest that Jesus himself may have been at Qumran. Was he not baptized by John and therefore strongly influenced by his ideas? Did he not fast in the desert, and, according to tradition, in a place not far from Jericho, only a few hours' distance from Qumran? As long as coincidences, guesses and hypotheses are *not* the raw material of history, it is better to admit our ignorance and to leave the rest to sensation-hunters.

Things had become unbearable in Judaea during the last years before the outbreak of the first great revolt of the Jews against the Romans in Palestine. Emil Schürer, the well-known historian of these times, says that it looks as though the Roman governors, who ruled the land from the death of Agrippa (A.D. 44) to the outbreak of war (A.D. 66), had made a secret compact to provoke the Jews to rebellion, according to a fixed plan. The Essenes may have led their own life, apart from the mass of the people, but when it came to insurrection they were in the thick of things, and even in the van. Josephus tells how a certain Essene called Johanan was made commandant of one of the districts into which the land was divided for the war. He also speaks of the heroic courage of the Essenes in enduring the torments which the Romans inflicted on them in the course of the war, to force them to 'blaspheme the lawgiver' (Moses) or to eat forbidden food. It is clear therefore that they did not stand aloof when the whole people was fighting for its freedom and when the whole national and indeed religious life was in danger.

The ruins of Qumran testify to the part played by the Essenes in the revolt. Revolt broke out in Jerusalem in May 66, and by September the rebels had full control of the

city. In November they defeated a Roman army and re-
entered Jerusalem in triumph. It goes without saying that war
against the overwhelming might of the Romans was bound
to end in disaster. The Romans could not be stopped even by
the most fanatical resistance. On the contrary, they were only
embittered by it. The first year of the war, 67, went badly
for the Jews. Galilee and the whole north of Palestine
were occupied by the Romans. In June 68 the Roman general,
later emperor, Vespasian, marched from Caesaraea on the
coast to the valley of the Jordan, Jericho and the Dead Sea.
'Mopping-up' operations went on *en route*, and Qumran was
not spared. Arrow-heads, and the marks of conflagration and
deliberate destruction point to the fact that the inmates of the
building fought it out.

Resistance cannot have lasted long, and though it was soon
broken, the Essenes must surely have displayed the courage
and endurance of which Josephus speaks.

According to all appearances, the brethren did their best
to bring their most important treasures into a place of security
as the enemy approached. They thought first of their sacred
books, which they had transcribed with such care, and read
and listened to with such pious sentiments. Qumran and the
environs must have contained hundreds of rolls, mostly
leather or parchment, some the cheaper and less durable
papyrus. They included texts of all the books of the Bible,
especially Deuteronomy, Isaiah and the Psalms. They also
included books like Tobias and Ecclesiasticus which some of
the Jews regarded as Sacred Scripture, though many did not.
For the most part, however, they were books belonging to the
private library of the brotherhood, composed by the founder
or his disciples or their likes, and reflecting their spirit. The
biblical works, and possibly others, were wrapped in linen
coverings and deposited four or five at a time in great jars,

which were carefully closed with a lid. The jars had been made in the Qumran potteries, and served also for household use. If they were made specially to hold books, no one thought it necessary to give them any special shape. When everything was packed, they took them to the neighbouring caves, to hide their precious treasures in the most inaccessible places available.

When the Roman troops had taken and fired the building, they proceeded to clean up in the vicinity and came upon some of the caves. They tore up the sacred books, but a number which escaped their destructive zeal survived, to be found in later times, as has been described in the beginning of this book. The damaged remains of the other books stayed where they were, to become the nests of wild beasts and the food of insects. The dust of ages covered them and they seemed to have passed into oblivion. The discoveries of 1947, however, started a treasure-hunt which raised the price of what had once seemed rubbish so high that before long a square centimetre of old unsightly leather could fetch a Jordan dinar (a pound sterling). Is this price too high? One should not be in too much of a hurry to say so. If an archaeological expedition had had to be fitted out to comb the desert as intensively as the Bedouin did, the total cost would perhaps have been higher.

After the devastation caused by the soldiers of the tenth legion, the building was just good enough to shelter a small desert outpost when some restorations had been effected. Since the Essenes had undoubtedly been all driven out, there would have been few inhabitants left in the region beyond the nomad Bedouin. Hence the building would have had to provide covering for only a small number of soldiers. The tower would, of course, have been put once more in a state of defence. The building, having lost its original purpose, was arranged differently. There was no longer need for so much storage space, and large rooms were partitioned into smaller ones, a thick wall was built across the inner courtyard, and the whole south-east portion of the building, to the east of this new wall, was left unoccupied and abandoned. A new oven was built, where bread was baked for the new occupants, a small garrison that lived in little rooms and kept watch on the surrounding country from the tower. At this stage, the building had lost its former character.

The coins found on the site indicate that the military occupation did not last very long, at a rough estimate no more than a few decades, i.e. till the end of the century. A military outpost in this part of the country became in the end super-fluous. The Jews had been completely crushed and peace and quiet had gradually returned to the whole land. Only nomads who did not threaten the power of Roman rule roved the desert, and there was no danger of their combining into important groups. The shore of the Dead Sea was as quiet as it had been before the Essenes settled there. Nomads passed by in the winter and brought their cattle to the spring of Ain Feshkha, birds of prey circled in the air with an occasional dismal cry, jackals prowled about, and in nearby Jericho their howl could be heard at night, like the distant whimper of small children.

Qumran was occupied on one more occasion. This was when the Jews of Palestine took up arms once more, in the year 132.

We are still not quite certain of the causes of this second revolt. Josephus was dead and he had no successor to write the history of the new rebellion. We have to rely on scattered and often late and vague accounts from various sources, Jewish, Christian and pagan. Two reasons are given: it appears that the Emperor Hadrian issued a strict prohibition of circumcision, which affected all who practised it, the Jews of course most of all. It appears also that he decided to carry out a new building scheme at Jerusalem, still the most famous city of the

East, and turn it into a completely heathen city. The emperor
had made a tour of the East to enhance his own glory and that
of the Empire; everywhere he had been greeted with pane-
gyrics; triumphal arches, some of which are still standing,
were erected in his honour, and he had promoted culture.
He wanted no doubt to do the same in Judaea, where, however, he did not take into account the mentality of the Jews
still living there. His procedure was due partly to ignorance,
partly to the typical colonial mind which disregards the
interests and wishes of the inhabitants when they do not coincide with its own. In the second revolt, the rebels were perhaps
even more determined and fanatical than those of the first.
Neither Jews nor Romans had forgotten the clash of sixty-five
years ago, and the Jews understood that the consequences of
the new revolt would be much more far-reaching. The
Romans sent one of their best generals, who came from
Britain to take command, but when the Jews were defeated
in open battle, they used every hole and hiding-place in the
land to carry on an embittered guerilla warfare, which cost
the Romans much time and trouble to suppress. The leader of
the revolt was a certain Bar Koseba, called by his Jewish
followers Bar Kochba, 'son of the star', a clear allusion to the
ancient prophecy of Balaam: 'A star shall arise out of Jacob,
a sceptre come forth from Israel; he shall crush the heads of
Moab, and be lord over all the sons of Seth' (Numbers 24: 17).
(The translation of the last phrase is uncertain. The sub-
stantive 'skull' may have stood at the beginning, but the
ancients took the word as a verb and explained it in various
ways; 'be lord over' agrees with the most ancient Jewish
tradition.)

Thus Bar Koseba was acclaimed as Messiah, and this
explains to some extent the great religious enthusiasm with
which the war was fought. Coins were struck at Jerusalem

bearing the legend: 'First year of the deliverance of Israel', 'second year of the deliverance of Israel', 'deliverance of Sion', etc. The revolt lasted three years and ended with the capture of Baither, seven miles south-west of Jerusalem, near the present Bittir, where Bar Kochba met his death, while the Jews were fighting to the last man. All Jews were now banished from Judaea, and were forbidden under pain of death to enter the city of Jerusalem or its adjoining territory. Three years of disaster, massacre and devastation, with the enslavement of tens of thousands, put an end to the Messianic dream.

In these years, 132–135, the old ruin of Qumran was occupied again, this time not by a Roman but by a Jewish garrison, as appears from the coins of the time found there, which were mostly Jewish. The Jewish soldiers must have made some repairs to the building, but the archaeologists have not yet found many traces of their activity.

Jewish guerillas also had outposts in the desert to the south of Qumran. The remains of one post have been discovered in the Wadi Muraba'at, where a rare piece of good fortune brought to light authentic letters personally signed by the leader of the revolt, Bar Koseba, alias Bar Kochba. The story sounded so unbelievable that Professor Zeitlin at once took pen in hand to assert that it was certainly untrue, while others expressed doubts, at least on the identification of Bar Koseba with Bar Kochba. Most of the letters have yet to be published, but a preliminary sample has been made available in the form of one letter, which runs as follows: 'From Simeon son of Koseba to Jeshua son of Galgola and the men of the stronghold: greetings. I call heaven to witness against me: if a single man of the Galileans whom you have rescued is missing, I shall put your feet in irons, as I did to the son of Aphlul. [S]imeon b[en Koseba, prince of I]s[rae]l.' The letters between brackets have been restored on the model of other epistles, while the translation of some words of the text is not certain, because there are gaps in it. Even so it is a precious document, which shows that Bar Kochba was a man of few words and energetic action.

The fort where ben Galgola was in command was in one of the most inaccessible places of all Palestine, eleven miles south of Qumran and fifteen miles as the crow flies south-east of Jerusalem. It is seven hours' good going from Bethlehem, along a route which in part is only passable on foot. There is a shorter way, but it is impassable after rain. At the end of the journey, after a tiring march and several back-breaking climbs, one reaches a place where the Wadi Muraba'at has become a deep and twisting ravine with steep walls almost six hundred feet high. Half-way up the northern face of the cliffs there are four caves close together, running back a few dozen yards, which can be reached only with extreme difficulty. This was ben Galgola's fort.

Bedouin had notified Father de Vaux of the place, in confidence, and he started explorations in the beginning of 1952. Much to the astonishment of the archaeologists, they discovered that the caves had been inhabited in the Chalcholithic Age, that is, before 3000 B.C. Other traces indicated also the Middle Bronze Age (2000–1600 B.C.) and some even the Iron Age (after 1200 B.C.). Most of the remains were from Roman times, some from the Early and Late Arabian.

The archaeologists found much to delight them in these caves, including rare museum pieces like a perfectly preserved cutting-instrument of wood, which must be more than five thousand years old and owes its soundness to the bone-dry atmosphere of the cave. Coins were also found, a number from the years A.D. 132–135. Ostraka too came to light (potsherds with writing on them), fragments of Hebrew, Aramaic and Greek documents, and even a Latin text. Very little of this last has survived; the experts say that it is certainly no earlier than the middle of the second century A.D. A number of letters are dated, all from the second century A.D. One document is a Jewish marriage contract, drawn up in Greek, from the seventh year of the emperor Hadrian (A.D. 124). Another Greek document contains the name of the emperor Commodus (A.D. 180–192). A Greek promissory note dates from A.D. 171. Then there are two other letters to Jeshua ben Galgola (compare the one cited above), one of which has been published. He is given the title of Camp Commander. There is an unpublished letter from Engaddi, and others where Simeon ben Koseba is 'in the camp', which probably means 'on active service'. Remains of biblical texts have also been found.

All the above-mentioned texts will be published in one volume at Oxford, and when the book appears we shall know more of the history of this nest of Jewish guerillas than we do now. At present what we can say is this: we do not know for certain that the position in the Wadi Muraba'at was being held before A.D. 132, because the documents of earlier date could have been brought to this outpost by someone who thought them worth keeping. From 132–135 some Jews lived there, and followed the precepts of their religion as well as they could under such difficulties. At any rate the remains of biblical books were part of the finds; the Pentateuch and the prophet Isaias are particularly well represented, and even phylacteries, that is to say, the little leather cases containing prayers which the Jews fastened on their forehead and left arm, as close to the heart as possible: the Gospel of St Matthew says that the scribes and Pharisees wore very big ones.

The stronghold was occupied again at a later date, towards the end of the second century. We shall not be able to say whether the occupants were Jews or Romans till all the texts are available. As regards the Jews, it is interesting to note that they corresponded with each other in Hebrew and not in

Aramaic. Was it nationalism that made them use the ancient language? Or was it not quite a dead language at the time? Probably not, because post-biblical Hebrew, of which the Muraba'at documents furnished specimens, contains forms which are only to be explained on the supposition that Hebrew remained a living tongue after biblical times. It also contains many words not represented in the cognate languages which can only derive from the ancient spoken language. This is not to say that Hebrew was the ordinary language of the men who were fighting for their freedom at Wadi Muraba'at. But they had kept up some Hebrew, by tradition, as has always been done in many Jewish communities, just as Latin survived among educated Christians to the end of the Middle Ages. It may well have been the only language they had learned to write in.

The finds at Wadi Muraba'at have no connexion with those of Qumran. The cliff-dwellers are completely distinct from the Essene community that lived on the shore of the Dead Sea. Had the Qumran brotherhood then ceased to exist? This is a new question in addition to those that have been raised in the course of this book. We cannot answer it. The later sect of the Karaites of which we have spoken earlier (see pp. 25 f. above) preserved customs which remind us of the brotherhood of Qumran, and their liturgical texts contain expressions which were also used at Qumran. As has already been said, some modern scholars explain this by supposing that the Karaites took a special interest in the manuscripts that were found in the region of Qumran in A.D. 800. If that is so it cannot be proved that the resemblances between Karaite and Qumranite are due to the persistence of old traditions in a section of Judaism itself. However that may be, it is true to say that when Qumran fell the Essenes disappeared from history, never to return.

4

THE VIEWS OF THE BROTHERHOOD

WHEN an association is founded, it aims at attaining a certain object, but does not necessarily demand of its members that they hold views which differ from those of outsiders. Associations may, however, be formed precisely on the basis of certain views which are not shared by others. A religious society so formed, which withdraws itself from common intercourse and is to some extent in conflict with its surroundings, may easily be a sect, and the Essene brotherhood of Qumran is often given this name. The first to use the term was Josephus, who speaks of the 'sects' of the Pharisees, Sadducees and Essenes, using the Greek word *Hairesis* which can also mean 'party, trend, school'. The word sect now has a derogatory sense, and anyone who uses the term generally dissociates himself from the group he is speaking of. For this reason, and in order not to anticipate what is to be said later, we have hitherto avoided the word as far as possible.

The Qumran brotherhood was, however, a typical sect. A writer on the sociology of religion, J. Wach, following a suggestion made elsewhere, says that a sect is usually formed when a fixed order of things is collapsing, which usually involves a transfer of political power and a new orientation of society. The sect is formed in an effort at healing and renewing society. Charismatic authority, that is the appeal to inspiration and inner enlightenment, is generally accorded a high place and is preferred to existing traditions. When a sect is once formed, it sometimes remains a small group, with a rigorously negative attitude towards outsiders. But it may also develop into a greater society, a fellowship which forms a church or the like. In the first case we have a typical 'sect'. Its members, no matter how few they may be, are sharply opposed to the group from which they sprang. They alone are right, the others are all wrong. As a rule, such a sect is born in the midst of conflict, and its members generally fight shy of their former co-religionists, at least in the beginning.

This description, taken for the most part from J. Wach (*Sociology of Religion*, 1944), fits the brotherhood of Qumran almost word for word. Its founder, or in any case its great organizer, was a man who felt himself to be inspired by the divine spirit, and claimed to know 'all the secrets' of the prophets by a direct illumination. He and his followers aimed precisely at a renewal of the people of Israel, a renewal that was to proceed from the small nucleus which they themselves formed. It was they who had kept the covenant which God had made with the forefathers, they were the true Israel, unlike the others who had departed from the covenant. We do not know what name they took, but they called themselves, among other things, 'children of light', in contrast to outsiders, Jews and non-Jews, whom they looked on as 'children of darkness'. The division between the two groups therefore runs not only through Israel but through the whole of mankind. The two groups are sharply opposed. In the very first column of the great Rule, one of the first things urged upon the brotherhood is that they must love the 'children of light' but hate the 'children of darkness'. Hebrew is a downright language, and the opposition between 'hate' and 'love' is not always as sharp as with us. Sometimes 'love' merely means 'prefer', and 'hate' is no more than 'disregard'. Thus when the Gospels say that we are to hate father, mother, brothers and sisters, and finally oneself, it means that their claims are to be disregarded in comparison to God and His claims. It is, however, beyond all doubt that 'hate' means more in the Rule than merely 'not choose', because it prescribes that the members 'must love all the children of light, each according to the portion granted him by God's decree, and hate the children of darkness, in accordance with the judgment of divine vengeance'. Such language can only be used with reference to people whom one positively dislikes, and whom one is determined in general to ignore. St Augustine says in his rule that one must love the sinner as much as one hates his sin, but that is the morality of the New Testament, and a very difficult one at that. To identify a man with his acts is a fault not confined to the primitive and inconsiderate: it is a deeply rooted inclination of human nature. Further, the group rejected certain traditions and practices which were general among the Jews, and opposed to them their own, as we shall see.

From all this it follows that the community of Qumran was a typical sect, or the headquarters of one. It is not quite correct to call it an 'order' in the way we speak of Christian monastic orders, or those of Islam. It was more than that, and it cherished the hope of one day, and even soon, embracing the whole of the old, corrupt Israel in a new kingdom of God. The group remained always very small. When Philo gives a number, he says 'more than four thousand'. In spite of this, it looked on itself as the small number of the elect to whom God's good purposes were confined, and it was convinced that with God's all-powerful aid it would win a splendid victory in the struggle with the whole world.

One reason, from a Christian point of view, why one hesitates to call the community of Qumran a sect is that in Christianity one is accustomed to sects which are distinguished from one another by points of doctrine and dogma. But the Jews never made so much of dogma as Christians: Sadducees and Pharisees got on quite well together, though the former denied an article that the latter believed, namely, the resurrection of the body. Between Essenes and Pharisees there would have been very little doctrinal differences, if any; yet the Essenes were further from the Pharisees than the Pharisees from the Sadducees. This is easily explained. It has been well said that when we speak of 'orthodox' Judaism, we do not mean orthodox in the Christian sense of correct doctrine, but orthodox in the special sense of correct practices. In other words, it is not a matter of the details of a set form of doctrines, but the precise manner of practising a religion, which for the good Jew meant the practice of the Law with its many precepts and prohibitions, and the carrying out of the prescriptions which were added later to ensure that the Law could be observed in all conditions of life. What distinguished the brotherhood of Qumran from their fellow Jews was above all the practice of certain customs, which may seem to us to be of very little or very subordinate importance, but which are of great significance to an Oriental, as for instance certain prescriptions bearing on ritual purity or the observance of a certain calendar of feast-days. The calendar could be crucial.

Doctrinally, the brotherhood of Qumran was completely based on Judaism. They read and used all the books of the Old Testament which are included in the Hebrew Bible of the present day. They certainly regarded the books of Moses, the prophets and the psalms as sacred and inspired, and there is no reason to think that they thought otherwise of the rest of the Bible. They also knew and read the sayings of Jesus ben Sirach (Ecclesiasticus), and the story of Tobias' marvellous travels, books which were accepted as 'biblical' by Jewish circles in Egypt. That they were also accepted as biblical by

Qumran is not clearly established, at least so far, but there certainly are reasons for thinking that they looked on Ecclesiasticus as canonical. The writer of this book did not derive his spiritual outlook from the same source as the Qumran sect. He differed from the Essenes in his view of the relation of life to death, since he spoke of death only as the end of life and had no doctrine to offer on the resurrection. And yet his book was read at Qumran.

Since they were convinced that the Teacher of righteousness was inspired by God to understand 'all the secrets of His prophets' they undoubtedly regarded his interpretation of them as a precious piece of divine revelation. We should not therefore be surprised if it should appear that they placed the writings of the Teacher, or his authentic sayings, on the same level as the Bible. But we are not certain, because it may well be that the community looked on the Bible as a definitive whole, unique in its genre, to which nothing could be added.

The Law of Moses was the most important part of the Bible, and the community took the view that it must be honoured and upheld in its entirety. Hence they were dominated by the thought that God had made a covenant with the forefathers and with the people, a covenant that all must live by. The community believed in God, in the election of the people, in the covenant, in the judgment of God who rewards the good and punishes the wicked, who wills that all live by the Law which He gave through Moses, not as a burden but as a privilege: and in all this they were typically Jewish, in no wise different from their fellow Jews. Yet there is unmistakable evidence that the community of Qumran held opinions which derived from a foreign source, though organically incorporated into the Jewish doctrine without coming into conflict with it. Such doctrines could also be supported by texts from the Bible which seemed to countenance them, so that on the whole they were regarded by those who professed them not as novelties but as authentic Judaism.

DUALISM

The most striking peculiarity of the doctrine of the brotherhood is its dualistic conception of the universe. The opinion or doctrine that two principles, one good and one evil, have confronted each other from the beginning and continue to struggle with one another for the lordship of the world and man, has been found among many peoples. According to the ancient Babylonians, the gods come forth from Apsu and Tiamat. The former is the ocean that was supposed to flow around the whole earth, the latter the sea, envisaged as a monster. When the god Marduk comes to be, he enters upon a mighty struggle with Tiamat, whom he overcomes and slays. Out of the sundered members of the monster's body he creates heaven and earth. Centuries before Christ, a doctrine was current in Persia that all existing things are to be referred to or derived from two primeval principles: the principle of good, with which the name of Ahura Mazda is primarily linked, and the principle of evil, known chiefly as Ahriman. What exactly was the Persian belief, and the precise form it took in different epochs of the national religion, is often difficult to define, but there can be no doubt that it consisted of a strongly dualistic tendency which opposed good and evil to each other as independent powers. Good and evil, also called light and darkness, or envisaged as such, were involved in perpetual strife, each striving to gain the mastery over the world and mankind.

This doctrine appears in another form as Zervanism, according to which Ahura Mazda and Ahriman were twin brothers, begotten by Zervan. But this view was not always held, and scholars are not yet quite clear as to who or what Zervan was. In later times, various forms of Manicheism transferred the dualism from the spiritual to the material sphere: the evil principle is matter in which the soul, an exile from the domain of light, is held prisoner.

This crudely dualistic view of matter was not the authentic doctrine of the great Persian prophet Zarathustra, better known under the name of Zoroaster in many quarters. He lived in the seventh century B.C. or earlier, and spoke in hymns and didactic poems which were recorded and given a place in the Avesta, the sacred book of the Persians. These hymns, the Gathas, still offer grave difficulties to the interpreter, as regards both language and doctrine. Very few scholars have studied them scientifically, so that our knowledge is not very advanced in this subject. However, some essential points of the doctrine of Zarathustra are sufficiently clear. For him Ahura Mazda is the supreme god, whose world is characterized by the opposition between good and evil which is everywhere present. This opposition is a spiritual one and is therefore represented as a conflict between two spirits. Ahura Mazda himself has chosen the good, men have yet to make this choice. Thus we read: 'Well then, in the beginning are the two spirits, who exist to the knowledge of all . . . as twins, the better and the evil, in thought, word and deed. And between these two the wise choose well, the foolish do not . . . Of these two spirits, the wicked strives to do the foulest things, but the most holy spirit, clothed in the firm heaven, has joined himself to righteousness, and all who desire to please the Wise Lord by good deeds have done in like manner.' Or again: 'I will speak of two spirits, of which the most holy, in the beginning of existence, did say to the destroyer: Neither our thoughts, nor our doctrine nor our spiritual powers, nor our choices, nor our words, nor our deeds, nor our consciences nor our souls are at one with one another.'

They who choose evil will be punished for it eternally, they who do what is good will enjoy immortality in the kingdom of light: 'Enduring darkness, miserable nourishment, bitter lamentation: to such an existence shall you be led, O wicked ones, by your conscience, for the sins you have committed. In the fullness of his own union with perfection and immortality, with righteousness in the Kingdom, shall the Wise Lord make all participate, who are sworn friends of the Good Thought in spirit and in deeds.' (Translated from the French of J. Duchesne-Guillemin, *Zoroastre*, Paris, 1948, Yasna 30: 3; 45: 2; 31: 21.)

It is quite clear that man can choose freely between good and evil; by this choice, he takes part in the strife in which the world is involved. If he hearkens to the good spirit and determines to follow him, he places himself among the good; if he takes the opposite decision, he joins himself to the wicked, the party of lies and darkness. The strife between the parties is brought to an end by a general judgment in which fiery flames of molten metal will separate the good from the wicked. In the blissful regions of light the good will be immortal and eternally happy, while the wicked will be punished for ever.

We find once more, in the writings of Qumran, a dualistic doctrine of two spirits which prompt men to good or evil, and of the consequent judgment. We read in the great Rule that the 'wise', that is, the initiated, who are to instruct others, must teach the sons of light 'according to their spirits', how the lot has fallen for mankind. God has created two spirits and allotted them to men to direct them in their conduct. 'They are the spirits of truth and of wickedness. All that is true comes from the dominion of light, all that is evil from the well-springs of darkness. Into the hand of the prince of lights is given the mastery over all the children of righteousness; they walk in the paths of light. Into the hand of the angèl of darkness is given all mastery over the sons of wickedness; they walk on the paths of darkness. When the sons of righteousness stray, this is due to the angel of darkness, and all their sins, misdeeds, wickedness and evil works are wrought at his command, according to the secret [decrees] of God, till His time is come' (Manual 3: 18–23). The text goes on to work out at length this theme of the two spirits, by giving an extensive list of all the good and evil deeds to which they inspire men. It seems too that 'the two spirits' mean groups or armies of spirits, good and evil.

Other texts tell us that the men of Qumran called the world they lived in 'the kingdom of Belial'. The name, which is also known from the New Testament (2 Corinthians 6: 15) often stands for the forces of wickedness as a whole, but Belial is also the chief of the wicked spirits. Michael is the leader of the good spirits. The word 'Belial' is ambiguous, because it is taken over from the Old Testament where it was constantly used to signify a person or a force that is intent on causing harm to others. Literally, the name seems to mean something like our 'good-for-nothing' and is often used to characterize wicked men more closely, especially the enemies of the pious. As often happens in human speech, the word took on a meaning in ordinary use which went beyond the component parts or the literal significance. 'Belial' appears as a baleful power intent on the destruction of others, especially men. He is so successful that most men listen to him and become thereby sons of darkness; the few who hearken to the suggestions of the good spirit(s) are the sons of light.

The agreement between this dualism and that of Zarathustra and the Persian religion is very noticeable. Various scholars have been so impressed by it that they concluded that the Jewish doctrine, which is later than the Persian, is inspired by the Persian dualism and therefore derives from it. Others have opposed this point of view, on the grounds that the dualism of Qumran may be very well regarded as a normal development and repercussion of ideas that can be found in the Old Testament. The notion of good and evil spirits is very ancient in the Bible, though the Old Testament is very reserved on this point, especially in the older parts. This reserve is generally explained as a precaution on the part of the sacred writer, who feared that the Israelites might one day begin to worship spirits on whose existence too much emphasis was laid. The later books of the Old Testament, especially those which do not belong to the Hebrew Bible, are more outspoken, say, in a story like that of Tobias, or even in the book of Daniel. Here the angels are often given names and they have very marked personalities. In the older books no names are mentioned—in the cult of a god or a spirit it was in practice necessary to know the name and pronounce it in his honour—and the angels often seem to be no more than gleams from another world with no individual personalities to distinguish them.

In an ancient text like 1 Samuel 16: 14 we read: 'the good spirit of Yahweh departed from Saul, and an evil spirit of Yahweh came to torment him'. In the first chapter of the book of Job, some centuries later, we find the well-known story of the evil spirit, called 'satan', that is, adversary, who appears on an evil day among the angels of God's court and receives permission from God to try his pious servant Job with all sorts of torments. The Old Testament writers and the Jews in general held that good and evil spirits were all subject to God, and if He permits the wicked spirit to torment a man, it is either to punish him, as in the case of Saul, or to give him an opportunity of displaying his virtue in all its splendour, so as to merit a glorious reward, as in the case of Job.

In the Qumran writings, and very particularly in the text quoted from them above, it is expressly stated that good and evil spirits have all been created by God. Man is free to choose and therefore God has offered him the choice between good and evil. The wicked spirit who spurs him so successfully to evil can do so only as long as the secret decree of God allows him. Then comes the general judgment, when the lordship is bestowed for good on the holy angels and the sons of light. Contrast the Persian religion where, especially in the later stages of its development, the dualism goes much deeper, because it is Ahura Mazda himself, the supreme God, who must choose between good and evil, and only then does he place himself at the head of all that is good.

The difference between the Persian view and that of Qumran is therefore undoubtedly profound: so much so, that Jewish opponents of the sect could not join issue with it on the grounds of faith, since it denied no article of Jewish doctrine. Furthermore, the teaching of Qumran could be of great help in explaining a number of texts from the Old Testament which spoke of good and evil spirits, and the attractiveness of the doctrine must have been due to a great extent to these biblical overtones. This, however, does not amount to a complete proof that the doctrine of the two spirits was entirely uninfluenced by notions of Persian origin. The development of Christian doctrine has likewise been aided in the course of centuries by the assimilation of notions which came from outside, and which stimulated it to reflect on its own principles, in order to formulate them more precisely and organize them systematically. The same process went on in Judaism, and there is no reason to think that the brotherhood of Qumran was exempt.

It is of course true, that the Jews, and those of Qumran most certainly, felt a strong repugnance to all that was heathenish, non-Jewish, in doctrine as in practice. We can hardly then suppose that they consciously adopted the doctrine of Zarathustra. But contact with the Persians, who adored a God of heaven like themselves, may have led them, not exactly to take over the Persian dualism, but to rediscover it, under another form, in their own religion. Dualism is after all a very seductive doctrine. At first sight, it explains the problem of the existence of evil much more easily than monism, which teaches that everything must go back to one principle—in monotheism, to the one creator and God. How is it possible after all that one and the same source should give rise to such opposites as good and evil, happiness and misery? Above all, how can a good Creator tolerate all the miseries of this world, my own in particular and the sufferings of the innocent, when He could eliminate them so easily! This question is as old as belief in a good God who has created the world and all that is in it, and it can be answered only by a faith that is founded on the rock-like conviction that God is just, that every man is a sinner and that the divine essence is an unfathomable mystery. The various forms of dualism offer an easier, though not more exact, solution.

Now we come upon this dualism once more as an essential part of the theology of the brotherhood of Qumran. It is expressed in terms which we seek for in vain in the Old Testament. The Bible speaks, to be sure, of good and evil spirits but they do not stand on either side of an unbridgeable chasm which also divides mankind into two groups. Furthermore, the opposing forces are not summed up as 'the spirit' of light and 'the spirit' of darkness, between which every man has to choose. Now it is the precise form in which a doctrine is expressed that must decide before all else the question of its dependence on other doctrines. In the case under review, the formal affinities seem so marked that it is difficult to exclude dependence of one on the other.

No complete answer can yet be given to the question of how and through what links the doctrine of Qumran is dependent on that of the Gathas. A direct dependence is not to be thought of. It would be grotesque to imagine the Teacher of righteousness studying the Gathas and taking his doctrine from them, even in modified and 'biblicized' form, nor has anyone suggested such a thing. But dualism was taken so much for granted in the Persian system that the Teacher or others of the same spiritual mould could well have heard of it, taken it over and incorporated it into their own religious system. It can hardly be an accident that the Rule makes so much of it: it was one of the doctrines peculiar to the brotherhood, and held in high esteem by them. The teachings of Moses were not explained in the Rule, because they were known to all. But the doctrine of the two spirits was in a different position. It has been asserted that Qumran borrowed it from the Zervanism of which we have spoken above. If so, God, the creator of good and evil spirits would be a counterpart of Zervan (Time?) who brings forth the twin brothers, good and evil, light and darkness. It is, however, quite unnecessary to go so far, firstly because the thought of God as the creator of all things was a generally accepted doctrine among the Jews at the time of the formation of the brotherhood; and secondly, because it is anything but probable that the sect would have promoted a god or a mythological being like Zervan to the place of Yahweh.

The same dualistic thinking as described above comes to the fore in another of the sect's books, namely, *The Rule of the War*, a work which was first published by Professor E. Sukenik of Jerusalem, under the somewhat romantic title of

The War of the Sons of Light with the Sons of Darkness. When the first specimens of this Rule were published, the newly founded State of Israel was engaged in a war with its Arab neighbours which was a matter of life and death. One gets the impression that Sukenik is suggesting a comparison between this modern war and the struggle announced in the first line of the old War Rule: the sons of Levi, Judah and Benjamin against the bands of Edom, Moab, Ammon, the Philistines and others. Naturally, the sons of light win.

The War Rule goes on to speak of a war of far greater dimensions which the sons of light, no longer based on the desert where they dwelt at first, but on Jerusalem and Judaea, will wage one day against all the nations of the earth. This war will last forty years, and will be directed against all the 'sons', i.e. peoples, of Shem, Ham and Japheth. The strategy of battle is briefly indicated, while the tactics of the armies of the sons of light are laid down at some length. Arms and accoutrement are prepared at Jerusalem, and then armies march out year by year to lands far and near, to bring the whole world under the rule of the sons of light, and to destroy for ever the power of Belial and his followers.

The Old Testament knows of only one war of aggression and conquest commanded by God: that in which the Jews gained possession of Canaan under the leadership of Moses and Joshua. David expanded his kingdom far outside its original limits, but this was not regarded as a holy war undertaken at God's command, even though Israel's borders were surely thought of as wider than Canaan (see Deuteronomy 1: 7). Apart from this, the holy wars of Israel were defensive in character. The prophets foresee a time to come at the end when Israel will reign over other peoples, they speak of Yahweh's punishing the heathen with the sword, but they do not speak of a great offensive war. In the last days, a spiritual revolution will take place in the hearts of all those who join themselves to Israel; the others are to be punished by God. The possibility that Israel will play a military role in all this is not definitely excluded; on the other hand, it is not expressly mentioned. The ideal of the future salvation is a time of peace, which will bring about conversion, knowledge of God, the dedication of life to His service.

Hence the thought of a general offensive war is not to be called biblical. It brings a new element into the notion of how the Kingdom of God is to be established on earth. We encounter such a conception in other religions, specifically in that of Islam. The *jihad* or holy war is one of the most important means of spreading the doctrine of the prophet, according to the Mohammedans. It is even their duty to wage it. The Assyrian kings marched out to conquest in the name of their god Assur, whose high priests they were and whose rule they were to extend by their conquests. Thus the idea of a holy war in which one takes the offensive is one which arose independently in various peoples. Hence there is no need to look far afield for a reason when one finds the thought in vogue at Qumran. But a foreign source can be indicated.

√ That the sons of light should look forward to waging a holy war on the whole world is connected with their dualistic mode of thought. Light and darkness according to their view were engaged in a perpetual struggle which was to end in complete victory for the light. This thought is basic in the War Rule and explains the aggressiveness of the sons of light. It also explains how this small group could think itself able to overthrow the whole world by force of arms in the short period of forty years. It is not to be ascribed entirely to chance that so great a part of this Rule in particular was preserved for future ages: the Rule was some of the best-loved literature of Qumran, and remains of a great number of copies have been found.

Philo once informed his readers that the Essenes were extraordinarily pacifist folk, who manufactured no weapons and therefore did not prepare themselves for war. Some modern scholars take this statement at its face value, and see in it a serious difficulty against identifying the Essenes with the Qumran brotherhood which produced the War Rule. But if one considers the objection carefully, it turns out to be of no consequence. No one would expect Philo to tell his Greek readers about the sort of war that the Essenes thought of waging in the future, even granted that he knew about it. His readers, instead of admiring the Essenes for their lofty way of life, would have begun to look on them as dangerous men. Besides, the holy war against the world belonged to dreams of the future which were to be realized only in later times: God would give the signal for it and surely also provide the weapons. Hence it is quite possible, and a very human trait, that the same man who refuses to have anything to do with weapons at the moment, could dream of God's providing him at a later date with weapons far more powerful than he could procure himself. Then again it may happen that men who preach pacifism as gently as any sucking-dove, may become roaring lions when they meet with violent opposition. Furthermore, the Essenes and the men of Qumran gave practical proof that they were ready and able to fight, when the highest interests of the nation and the group were at stake. When war with the Romans came in 66–70, they did not refuse to join the ranks of battle.

IMMORTALITY

Another and very important belief shared by the Essenes and the brotherhood of Qumran was the conviction that the sons of light would be received into the ranks of the angels after death, to enjoy perpetual happiness among them. One of the Qumran psalms, which has been made public for some years, expresses this as follows:

> I will praise thee, O Lord,
> because thou hast redeemed my soul from the pit,
> and out of the destruction of the underworld thou hast led me up
>   to an eternal height.
> I walk in a boundless plain
> and I know that there is hope for him whom thou hast created
>   from dust,
> unto the eternal assembly.
> Thou hast cleansed the sinful spirit from great evil
> to place him in the array of the host of the holy ones,
> to set him among the congregation of the sons of heaven.
> Thou hast granted to man a lot perpetual
> along with the spirits of knowledge
> to praise thy name with them
> and to announce thy wonders in the sight of all thy works.

The thought of a blessed immortality and of an eternal happiness reserved for the pious among the angels may be said to be foreign to the Hebrew Old Testament. The ancient Israelite looked for blessedness not in the after-life, but on earth. God made man in order that he might serve him on this earth, and rewards him for this service with length of days, much progeny and rich possessions. Man does not entirely cease to exist at death, but he is finished with happiness when this life is over. His personality is not quite extinct, but the Old Testament does not use a noun in the singular for what survives. The plural, *rephaim*, meaning 'the weak, exhausted, limp' occurs a few times, and indicates the faint shadows of human personality which survive in the underworld. These *rephaim* are very much less than what we would call 'souls': they are the debris of what once were men. They dwell in the underworld, which is represented as a tomb of enormous proportions, where both good and bad languish and lament for ever. Hence death is the worst that can come upon a man, and a premature death is the punishment *par excellence* of the sinner. This was still the mind of Ecclesiasticus, as late as the beginning of the second century B.C. As all men do some time or other, he thought of his own death, and as a sage, he reflected on the death of all men. Death is bitter, he philosophized, except for the man who has known only misery in this life; for him it is the lesser of two evils. Hence he wrote in a sombre moment:

O death, how bitter is the remembrance of thee
for the man who dwells tranquilly in his house,
for the man without troubles who is prosperous in all things,
and that is yet able to gather the fruits of joy . . .
O death, how welcome is thy portion
to the poor man whose strength is wasted
to the man who totters and falls foul of everything,
whose life is a burden and who lacks all hope . . . (Ecclesiasticus
41: 1f.).

After unbosoming himself to this effect, the sage goes on to say that man must nevertheless relinquish everything at death, since God has so disposed.

The thought of death loses its sting for the first time in the Old Testment when the doctrine of the resurrection appears, which is only found in a clear and unambiguous manner in the latest books. The prophet Ezechiel appears to have envisaged the possibility of the resurrection of the body when he saw in vision a field of dry bones and heard God ask him: 'Son of man, shall these dead bones live again?' (Ezechiel 37: 3). Unable to answer, he says: 'Lord Yahweh, thou knowest.' Later God reveals to him that the bones were not really human skeletons, but a symbol of the people of Israel, which while in exile was in a state that could be called 'death', but which was to rearise. Many commentators on the Old Testament adduce various texts in which the doctrine of the resurrection of the dead is supposed to appear, but these can mostly be explained in more than one way. The first text which speaks clearly and definitely of the resurrection is Daniel 11: 2, dating probably from around 165 B.C. and so part of the latest of Old Testament writings. In the second book of Maccabees, half a century later, if not more, we read that the seven Maccabean martyrs sustained mutilation and death courageously in the conviction that their members would be restored to them whole and entire at the resurrection (2 Maccabees 7: 9, 11, 14).

How they pictured the life after the resurrection, we do not know, but it looks very much as if they thought of it as a continuation, perhaps in a modified form, of this earthly life. We are not quite clear about the form which the doctrine of the resurrection took at Qumran. Josephus says of the Essenes that they were convinced of the corruptibility of the body and of the immortality of the soul. At death, the soul escapes from the corpse as though from a prison and flies aloft to reach the bright ether beyond the great ocean that encircles the world. There no rain or snow, or cold or heat can harm it, and the soft cool air that rises from the ocean is its perpetual refreshment. Josephus compares this view with that of the Greeks, and hence we must regard his description in the same light: it corresponds to Greek rather than Essene ideas. If we take his words at their face value, they exclude the resurrection, because if the body is looked on as a prison, the soul cannot be made any the happier by being reincarcerated in it. The expression was probably a concession to Josephus' Greek readers, who, as he knew well, and as the apostle St Paul experienced when addressing the Areopagites, found the notion of a bodily resurrection ridiculous. The resurrection was denied by the Sadducees, but asserted by the Pharisees, and it became one of the most important doctrines of Judaism and Christianity.

It may be that the resurrection was taken so much for granted at Qumran that they did not give it any particular emphasis. One can even point to a text in the Qumran psalms which says that on the day of judgment all the sons of truth shall 'awake'. But the fact is that the thought of a blessed immortality appears to have pushed the notion of a bodily resurrection into the background. A scholar like T. Gaster seems to be unable to find either immortality or resurrection in the Qumran texts, but he is certainly over-critical.

The hope of being received among the angels (at what period of the world is not said) supposes that more remains after death than a mere shadowy fraction of human existence; what is released from the body must be something in the nature of a 'soul' in which the human personality persists and which has the status of *spirit*. There is no other possibility. This is clearly proclaimed in one of the books of the Greek Bible, the so-called Wisdom of Solomon, which was written in Greek, in the first century B.C. in Egypt, and which some serious scholars hold to be connected with the Qumran writings. Here we find the well-known words: 'The souls of the just are in the hands of God, no trouble can vex them. In the eyes of fools it seemed as though they died, men looked on their end as a calamity, and their passing as the end of everything. Though it seemed indeed to men that they were punished, yet it is immortality that awaits them, and after brief affliction they are richly rewarded' (Wisdom 3: 1–5).

There is little support for this way of thinking in the Hebrew Old Testament. How did it reach Qumran? Zarathustra spoke of the 'blessed regions' which Ahura Mazda has filled with light, and whither the pious are admitted as the reward of their good deeds, to enjoy his presence and sing his praises eternally. Long after Zarathustra, the Persian religion still cherished the thought, and it is possible that the Qumranite view is connected with it, because it was well known to Judaism in general and passed over from Judaism into Christianity. Not only the Persians but the Egyptians and many other ancient peoples believed in the immortality of the soul, so much so that a Netherland scholar, G. van der Leeuw, could write: 'The Hebrews were almost alone in the ancient world in facing death in all its ruthlessness.' The thought of survival after death and a happy hereafter tallies with the deepest yearnings of man's nature. No wonder we meet it again and again in the religions of mankind, as also at Qumran. The question of dependence on Persian lines of thought could only be solved by showing that the doctrine is expressed in specifically similar terms in both religions. It is very difficult, however, to put one's finger on such similarities, all the more so because the Qumranites were certainly not *directly* influenced by Zarathustra or his writings.

It seems to me that the (moderate) dualism of the Qumran brotherhood made it easy for them to accept the idea of immortality or helped them to develop it. When immortal spirits exercise so decisive an influence on the lot of man, and strive so hard to win men to their side during their earthly lives, for good or evil, the thought of being received into their company after death cannot be very far away. It can take place after the general judgment, or earlier. Furthermore, the men of Qumran could appeal to biblical texts. There are at least three texts in the Old Testament psalms which contain expressions capable of being interpreted as promises of a future life of blessedness for the pious in God's presence:

For thou dost not abandon my soul to the underworld,
Thou dost not permit thy pious servants to see the pit.
Thou makest known to me the path of life,
thou dost satiate me with joy before thy face (Psalm 16: 10f.).
God shall free my soul
from the power of the underworld, for he shall take me up
(Psalm 49: 15).
But I am always by thee,
thou hast taken me by the right hand,
thou dost lead me by thy counsel,
and after [...] thou dost take me up (Psalm 73: 23, the brackets indicate a practically unintelligible word).

The meaning of these verses is much debated. At first sight they seem in fact to speak of a life with God in the hereafter, and many commentators take this meaning from them. But Hebrew style is fond of imagery and hyperbole, that is, strong, crude, seemingly exaggerated ways of putting things. Many commentators think that this is the case here, and that the authors of the three texts in question are simply expressing their conviction that God will preserve them from untimely death and so grant them the happiness of being with Him on earth, either in spirit or in the temple. They point out that it would be strange if such a weighty doctrine as that of immortal blessedness were to be so briefly and lightly touched on in these psalms, without the emphasis which it merits, particularly as it is not heard of elsewhere, either in the psalms or the rest of the Hebrew Old Testament.

It is hard to decide which side to take. Two things, however, are certain. Even if the psalmists do not state it as their conviction in the three texts in question that they are to be eternally happy with God, they testify at any rate that life with

God is for them the supreme happiness. It stands to reason that this includes the desire that such happiness never cease. On the other hand, it is clear that the Teacher of righteousness, or the brotherhood of which he was the great prophet, could have found support for their own views in the three texts from the psalms, especially the first. It is even possible that close reading and meditating of these texts might have brought about the conviction that the doctrine of immortal blessedness, possibly already known from other sources, was contained in these texts. Here again they would be building on Old Testament ideas.

PREDESTINATION

The concept of predestination is one that frequently occurs in the writings of Qumran. God has a plan for the world, and He puts it into execution. He chose long ago the people of Israel to serve Him, but most of the Israelites were unfaithful, and now the circle of the elect is in fact restricted to the little group of 'the sons of light'. They it is that are called to happiness, all the others will be condemned by God and lost for ever. The pious attribute all their good fortune to God, as is affirmed in the very first of the Thanksgiving Psalms, where the psalmist proclaims himself to be nothing but a sinful being; God has even determined the words of the pious before they were uttered. The psalm which is added to the great Rule as a sort of concluding hymn, speaks as follows:

> For the way that a man goes is not his own,
> man does not dispose his own steps,
> for God ordains it;
> if one does well, that comes from Him!
> Through His wisdom all things came to pass
> and all that is has been determined by His plan,
> and without Him it does not come to be (Manual 11: 10–11).

It may be inferred that the author of the psalm taught the doctrine of a general predestination. One could say that just as men's good deeds come one and all from God, so too God is responsible for their absence; God chooses out His own and ordains them for happiness; from which it follows that He leaves the others in the lurch and they go to perdition.

Such a conclusion follows indeed from the above and similar texts, but only if one is to take it that the Teacher of righteousness and his followers thought everything out logically and hoped thereby to penetrate the divine mystery. We must, however, remember that the relation between divine help and grace on the one side, and human act on the other, has always been an awesome mystery to the believer. In Christianity, both Catholic and Protestant theologians have been preoccupied by the problem and both sides have tried to cast light on it from many different angles. The finest theologians have sharpened their wits on it, without ever reaching an agreement. God is all-powerful and without Him nothing can happen and man also can do nothing; but man is free in his actions, and God holds him responsible for his sins. How is all this to be harmonized?

The Old Testament is emphatic, and repeatedly so, in stating that Yahweh, the God of Israel, is above all just. He can never do anything unjust, because He loves good and hates evil. At the same time we read that 'Yahweh hardened the heart of Pharaoh, so that he could not let the Israelites go' (Exodus 4: 21, etc.). And it is said of Israel's king that his heart is in Yahweh's hand like the water of a canal which a man has dug and can direct at will (Proverbs 21: 1). What is true of the heart of the king is certainly true of all men. But if their hearts are thus in Yahweh's hand, where is man's independence? Besides these two texts, others could be quoted to the same effect from the Old Testament. But they are, however, very rare: as if the Israelites were faced with a mystery of which they would rather not speak.

When the modern theologian is trying to present the mysterious divine process which we are speaking of, he uses terms that make some understandable sense and says that God does not will what is evil, but that He does will the permission of evil. This permission is not a purely negative thing, as if God held Himself aloof and had absolutely nothing to do with it. It is something positive, and indeed positive in a measure that passes understanding. In human affairs, it is easy to understand how a man could positively will 'not to hinder something harmful' in order to prevent greater evil. So for instance the prudent lawgiver deliberately refrains from legislating against every possible misdemeanour, because too many legal prescriptions would lower the law in people's estimation and restrict liberty unduly: the remedy would be worse than the disease. So too one can conceive of God's permitting evil for the sake of a higher good, and the idea is correct. Sometimes this higher good can be indicated, for example, respect for human freedom; but frequently it escapes us. However, while men are restricted to certain means for attaining their ends, God suffers from no such restrictions, and this is what creates most of our difficulties in understanding the divine mode of action. The sincere believer does not even try to, and bows his head before the divine mystery.

The ancient Israelite had no clearer insight into the divine act which the modern theologian describes as 'a positive refusal to hinder'. He expressed it in his own terms, and spoke of the 'hardening' of Pharaoh's heart, indicating thereby that God had something to do with it, but seeing no way of reconciling His hatred of sin with the seemingly contradictory act

of 'hardening'. Ecclesiasticus pondered the problem and wrote
as follows:

> Say not: my fault comes from God,
> because He has not done that which He hates.
> And do not say: He has made me stumble,
> because He has no need of the evil-doer.
> All that is abominable is hateful to Yahweh,
> He guards all them that fear Him from its touch.
> God created man in the beginning
> and left him in the hand of his own counsel:
> if you will, you keep His commandments,
> and perform His will loyally.
> Water and fire are poured out before you,
> stretch out your hand to whichever you choose.
> Life and death are put before man,
> what he desires is granted him.
> The wisdom of Yahweh ranges far and wide,
> He is strong and mighty and sees all things.
> God's eyes regard His works,
> all that a man does is observed by Him.
> He has not commanded man to sin,
> He gives no leave or licence to do evil things
>
> (Ecclesiasticus 15: 11–20).

This is how a pious Jew thought of the matter, in the beginning of the second century B.C. and his book was part of the
devotional raeding of Qumran, as the remains of it found
there testify. That does not mean that the people of Qumran
held the same views as he did, but it may help us to understand
the views which were current there.

At Qumran, they were convinced that man is, in principle,
free. The spirits of good and evil which God has placed in his
midst are 'equal', as it says in the great Rule in the passage
concerning the two spirits; and they strive in (less correctly:
'for') the heart of man. Man can therefore decide which spirit

he will listen to; once he has made the decision, the good he does is a result of the help and the suggestions of the good spirit, ultimately, therefore, the work of God, while evil is the consequence of the promptings of the evil spirit. Nowhere is it said that the decision can only be taken once; men can repent and be converted, just as they can also fall away after a time. The Rule gives at any rate directions for those who wish to join the brotherhood, fixes penalties for transgressors and excludes certain traitors from the community for good. It follows that it is not God but the man himself who is responsible when he sins and he will one day be punished for it by God.

Such sentiments in the Hymns as 'man does not dispose his own steps' are always uttered with reference to the pious; the pious who have chosen aright receive further help from God. One thinks spontaneously of St Paul, writing to the Romans: 'To will is present with me, but to accomplish that which is good, I find not' (Romans 7: 18. And see below, p. 119; and ch. 7). Further, one must not lose sight of the fact that the hymnic style, by its very nature, and completely in keeping with the Old Testament psalms, leads to an extremely emphatic preoccupation with man's weakness and his impotence apart from God. In the psalms of the Bible, the singer often calls himself a poor, miserable, worthless sinner, who is in mortal danger from wicked and powerful enemies and in such straits that only God can help him. In the East, and indeed elsewhere, the beggar who appeals to the sympathy of his fellow men makes himself out as poor and miserable as he can. The Israelite who sought God's favour did just the same before God. The psalmist of Qumran stresses, therefore, in a perfectly understandable manner his own impotence, his own sinfulness and the omnipotence of God without which he can accomplish no good work. He goes undoubtedly a step further than the authors of the biblical psalms, but along the lines they laid down. And it is altogether in keeping with the style of these poems that nothing is said about what man can do of himself; under no circumstances is any stress laid on this.

God is furthermore a 'God of knowledge'. He has foreseen all the deeds of men, and He has used this prescience to lay down His unalterable plan for the world. This too we can read in the Hymns, and it is not a complete novelty that they offer us. The biblical book of Ecclesiastes had at any rate already pointed out the unalterable course of things as something ordained by God which men cannot modify. Ecclesiastes speaks of things in general, while the Thanksgiving Psalms seem to apply his assertion to all particular events and to the course of human life.

According to Josephus, the Essenes held that an irresistible fate controlled human destiny; the Sadducees repudiated this doctrine and the Pharisees held an intermediate position, admitting that some human actions were decided by fate, while others were not.

When Josephus speaks of fatalism, his language is as inexact as when for instance he speaks of Moses writing hexameters. The hexameter is a Greek metre which does not occur in Hebrew poetry, a fact of which Josephus was perfectly well aware. But he could not explain the real structure of Hebrew verse to readers who did not know Hebrew, so he spoke only of 'hexameters'. He is adopting the same technique when he speaks of fatalism as a doctrine held by the Essenes. The heathen doctrine of blind fate was in fact unknown to the Jews, because it was excluded by their faith in the foreknowledge of God. The Jews thought of providence where the heathens thought of fate. Now, the more completely the Jews ascribed events to divine 'predestination', the more closely they approximated, it would appear, to heathen views of fate. This is how we must understand what Josephus says of belief in 'fate' among Sadducees, Pharisees and Essenes.

In their view of foreknowledge and predestination, the Essenes did not stand quite alone in Judaism. Every Jew took it for granted that God knows everything beforehand, including the free actions of men. His plan for the world was based on this knowledge. About the difficult question of how God's foreknowledge and divine decrees were to be reconciled with man's freedom, opinions were divided. According to the Mishna (first and second century A.D.), the Talmuds (third to fifth century) and other ancient Jewish writings, the rabbis offered various solutions. Some said that God may sometimes be moved by the prayer of the just to alter His decrees. Others thought that the divine predestination took as its guiding line the good and evil works which were foreseen by God and performed entirely by men themselves. Others again said: 'All is in God's hands, except the fear of God'; or, putting it in another way, 'Each one's lot is fixed, except whether he will be just or unjust.' For the last view, Deuteronomy 10:12 is invoked: 'And now, Israel, what else does Yahweh your God *ask* of you, except that you fear Yahweh your God, so that you obey all His precepts, love Him, and serve Yahweh your God with all your heart and all your soul?' They argued that what God 'asks' of men must be within men's power.

SINFULNESS

As regards human nature, the Qumranites were strongly convinced of man's sinfulness. Many expressions and utterances in the Hymns seem to be no more than a broad development of the saying of Genesis: 'The thoughts of the heart of man are evil from his youth' (Genesis 8: 21). Experience confirms this and the writers of the Hymns have had painful proof of it in themselves:

> I belong to sinful mankind
> to the community of sinful mortals.

My misdeeds, my trespasses, my sins
and the badness of my heart
belong by right to the fellowship of worms
and to those who roam in the darkness (Manual 11: 9–10).

The thought is perfectly in keeping with the Old Testament, but the striking thing is that the writers of the Hymns do not appeal to their (relative) innocence, as happens in the biblical psalms from time to time. Thus the consciousness of their own sinfulness suppressed the thought of their own perfection. For that matter, any perfection in man is ascribed completely to God's doing in the Hymns, so that the writer has no reason to appeal to it. The fact of universal sinfulness is explained in the Old Testament by the sin of our first parents; original sin is represented as the first sin, which had dire consequences for all men. In Christianity we find the doctrine that the whole of human nature is affected by a mysterious guilt, which everyone participates, by the fault of Adam, as he comes into existence. This concept is not yet found in the writings of Qumran.

The Qumran Hymns proclaim again and again that man is a sinner and that he is punished by God for his sins. All the good he does comes from God; by his own strength he can do nothing. From the passage about the two spirits in the great Rule we can deduce that man chooses freely between the good and the evil spirit; once he has made his choice, the spirit he has chosen makes him behave well or ill. If one combines this thought with that of the Hymns, one comes to the conclusion that man is responsible for his own deeds, even though he can do no good of himself. Thus the justice of God is maintained. How all this is possible to God remains a mystery.

GNOSIS?

It would be too difficult in these pages to go deeply into the question of the relation of the Qumran texts to what is called *gnosis* (Gnosticism). The Greek word means 'knowledge', and in the century about the beginning of our era is often used of a very special type of knowledge, that of secret, revealed, supernatural and preternatural truths which certain groups of initiates were in possession of. So understood, the concept is very elastic and there were various forms of gnosis in the ancient world. St Paul speaks repeatedly of gnosis in his Epistles and the most ancient Christians proclaimed theirs as the true 'gnosis', the true knowledge of the mysteries revealed by God.

The discussion of the gnostic or otherwise character of the Qumran writings has remained fruitless so far in many respects, for lack of precision in determining the meaning of the words 'gnosis' and 'gnostic' and the type of historical phenomenon envisaged. Although some scholars thought otherwise in the beginning, it is becoming clearer every day that the Qumran community stood outside the particular trend in the practice of gnosis which is called Gnosticism, and which flourished chiefly in the second and third Christian centuries. The doctrine professed at Qumran was too well and truly Jewish to be called gnostic by us, that is, in the technical and historical sense in which the word is ordinarily used. If even so the Greek word *gnosis* has been applied to some passages from the Qumran writings, this is due to certain affinities which will be briefly described or pointed out in the following pages.

The Teacher of righteousness was conscious of having received revelations from God concerning 'secrets' which had hitherto been hidden. God had even imparted to him 'all the secrets of His servants the prophets'. These secrets are not supernatural truths about the essence of God which must always remain incomprehensible for men, like the Christian mystery of the Trinity. They are divine decrees, intimated by the words of the prophets and now become clear to the initiates who have received revelation concerning them. God fixed His plan for the world from the beginning, even before anything was created. He did not immediately make His plan known, since the time was not yet ripe. This view of things is merely the transference into the divine plane of what happens on earth. A king or military leader takes decisions in his secret council concerning measures to be taken at some future time, but which are only made public and put into force when their time has come. What an earthly king does on a small scale, God does on a large scale. The apostle St Paul speaks in the same sense of 'the revelation of the mystery, which was kept secret for ages, but is now made known by the writings of the prophets at the command of the eternal God' (Romans 16: 25–26), namely, the eternal plan of God, to call the heathen to salvation besides the Jews. This was already to be read in the prophets, but is only now become perfectly clear. The apostle revealed still another 'mystery' to the Romans: the divine decree that Israel, as yet unbelieving, is to come to belief in the Gospel, when first the mass of the heathens have accepted it (Romans 11: 25–26). 'Mysteries', if taken in this sense, are no longer mysteries when they are revealed and known to everybody. Besides these, there is the mysterious, unfathomable essence of God, a mystery that was never made known to man, at Qumran or elsewhere. God's providence, too, man cannot grasp completely; it is only possible in so far as God grants insight.

Clearly, the men of Qumran, and Essene circles in general, claimed to know more than others about the divine plan for the world. According to Josephus, the Essenes had to promise to keep their books and the names of the angels secret. Certain passages in the great Rule indicate that a certain secrecy was observed with regard to outsiders, but what precisely was kept secret is not clear. There is, however, no reason for regarding this secrecy as something quite peculiar and distinctive in the group's attitude. Since they were convinced at Qumran that God had taken His own into His confidence in a very special way, it is only natural that they preferred not to speak about it to others who refused to accept this revelation.

THE TEACHER OF RIGHTEOUSNESS

In the eyes of the brotherhood, the Teacher of righteousness had the standing of a great prophet, through whom God has made known His purposes to the members of the community and to all who joined it. This naturally implied obligations, and to all appearances these were laid down, along with the old, in a 'new covenant'. Some scholars have also asserted, or still assert, that the *person* of the Teacher occupied an important place in the beliefs of Qumran, in a manner comparable to the person of Jesus Christ in Christianity. If one considers the matter dispassionately, it is precisely here that the greatest difference between Essenism and Christianity becomes apparent. If one may speak of a central figure in the beliefs of Qumran, it was Moses and not the Teacher who held their attention. To be sure, the Teacher was an intermediary between God and his own followers, he was the instrument of divine inspiration, but he did not occupy a central place in their belief. His name has not yet been discovered in the Qumran writings, ancient writers like Josephus and Philo do not know him, and his disciples did not name themselves after him, as far as we know. (That he was called Zadok, and that his disciples were called 'sons of Zadok' on that account, has been maintained by only a few writers.)

The Damascus Document states that all who live according to the Law, and at the same time listen to the voice of the Teacher of righteousness, confess their sins and do what the

Teacher commands, shall one day rejoice, display their power to other mortals and receive from God forgiveness of their sins (Damascus Document 20: 27–34). The passage ends with the words: 'They shall see His [God's] salvation [i.e., they will be saved by God] because they had confidence in His holy name.' The Teacher is a prophet, and he utters the words which God has put in his mouth, but salvation comes from God, as the words just quoted make clear. In the Habacuc Commentary the famous words: 'The just lives by his faith [or: his fidelity]', (Habacuc 2: 4), are explained as follows: 'The exposition of this refers to all in the house of Judah who keep the Law; where they are judged God shall save them for the sake of the labours they bore and their confidence in [or: belief in, i.e. fidelity to] the Teacher of righteousness' (Habacuc Commentary 8: 1–3). Obviously, the expression 'confidence' or 'belief' (the Hebrew word *emunah* is best translated 'confidence', 'loyalty'; 'belief' is not quite the same thing) is used here simply because it occurs in the biblical text of Habacuc which the commentator is explaining. It is also clear that this belief does not regard the *person* of the Teacher but the *words* which he utters in the name of God. Belief in God and belief in the words of the Teacher coincide, since God put the words on the lips of the Teacher.

A speaker in the Thanksgiving Psalms tells of the revelations which he has received from God and passed on to men; God, he says, has made his lips a spring of living water which became a great stream flowing out in all directions and bringing fertility and blessing everywhere (Hymns 8: 1ff.). Elsewhere he (or someone else?) says that God has made him a father to those who are the object of God's loving kindness, a guardian to those who are a sign (to others) and who have taken in his words as a suckling drinks milk at the breast (Hymns 7: 20f.). This is vigorous language, and many have suspected that it is uttered by the Teacher himself. If so, it indicates in him a strong conviction of being God's envoy. Isaiah and other prophets complained that their words were not listened to; the speaker in the Hymns, on the contrary, rejoices at having found so many to follow him. The difference is palpable: the great prophets address themselves to the whole people and gain a hearing only from a few; the Teacher is primarily the leader of a group, a sect, and is glad of it.

Some scholars have so exaggerated the role of the Teacher as to say that in the eyes of his associates he was the Messiah, the long-awaited deliverer and redeemer of Israel and the world. There is little or nothing of this in the texts; the theory depends to a great extent on texts that were mistranslated when study of them was only in its infancy. There are, however, a number of passages where the Teacher is expressly distinguished from the Messiah and which therefore contradict the above-mentioned theory.

It is now clear that the men of Qumran awaited the coming of two 'Messiahs' (i.e. anointed ones): one from 'Aaron' and one from 'Israel'. The meaning of these expressions, which seemed strange at first, has been clarified by later research and the discovery of new texts. The Qumran sect, being a priestly brotherhood, put the priest (meaning the high priest, the head of the priesthood) above the secular prince in the happy kingdom that was to come. 'Aaron and Israel' had much the same meaning for the members of the group as 'clergy and laity' has for us (all priests were considered descendants of Aaron). No doubt they also believed that a Messiah of the race of David would come at the head of his people. He was, however, to take second place in the restored Israel, because the high priest was regarded as the most immediate representative of God in a future society directed by God.

After this brief description of some of the most striking

points of doctrine on which Qumran differed from the current thought of the Jews, we shall say a few words about some marked differences in the practices of the brotherhood, which had far more to do with the development of a sectarian and separatist way of life than their purely 'theological' views. Judaism, then as now, has always been very adaptable in its theology, provided the accepted fundamental principles of Scripture and Tradition were not menaced. Pharisees and Sadducees prayed and offered sacrifice in the one temple, while the Essenes held aloof. How did this come about?

CLEAN AND UNCLEAN

The author of the Damascus Document complains that in his day the sanctuary, the temple of Jerusalem, was being polluted by the priests because they neglected the rules for ritual purity which the writer regarded as divine prescriptions. He held, for instance, that the text of Genesis 1: 27 implied a prohibition of a second marriage; widows and widowers were therefore obliged to persevere in that state of life. He also held that an uncle was forbidden to marry his niece, on the basis of Leviticus 18: 13, 'Thou shalt not mate with thy mother's sister, for she is thy mother's flesh and blood.' This actually forbade only marriage with an aunt, but from the motive adduced, 'she is thy mother's flesh and blood', that is, her closest kin, the rigorists of Qumran concluded that marriage with any of the direct descendants of the aunt was also forbidden. Official Judaism did not accept this view, though it had some success elsewhere, as it is found among the Samaritans, the Karaites and the Falasha or Abyssinian Jews. Because one must be pure to offer a pure sacrifice, and because many priests married more than once in their lifetime or even married a niece, the temple was polluted by their presence and the sacrifices they offered were impure! The Essenes refused to co-operate in such doings, and they therefore set themselves to wait for better days, when their word would be law in the temple. In the meantime they drew up regulations which would be valid on the great day, which may be read in the great War Rule. This makes it perfectly clear that the Essenes had broken with the temple cult under the given circumstances but that they did not oppose the sacrificial services on principle, as various scholars thought until recently.

THE CALENDAR

Many readers will have wondered whether these difficulties against partaking in the temple worship, which seem to us exaggerated, if not ridiculous, were really conscientious objections or only a pretext to avoid participation. The question is not easy to answer, but at all events we must try to rid ourselves of our own point of view in the matter, and not try to solve it on the basis of what would seem reasonable to us. Matters of ritual were of great importance to the Jews of the time, as they still are to many Orientals. At Qumran, furthermore, the significance of ritual purity was pushed to the limit; the community stood or fell by it, so to speak. The brotherhood of Qumran also departed from the usages of the rest of the Jews in another matter of ritual, none other than that of the calendar. Originally the Jewish year was divided into twelve months of equal length, corresponding to the duration of the circuit of the moon. As in its journey round the earth it takes the moon about twenty-nine and a half days to come back to the same point in relation to a given place on earth, and as months of twenty-nine and a half days are hard to work with, the length of the month alternated between twenty-nine and thirty days. Hence the year, a lunar year, lasted 354 days and was short eleven days, more precisely eleven and a quarter, each year. From the time of Mohammed, the Mohammedan dating is done by these lunar years, as a result of which the civil and religious feast-days of the year pass from one season of the year to another. Ramadan, the month in which Mohammedans fast, falls in one year in the summer; some years later it will be in the spring, later on again in winter, and still later, in autumn. This is obviously attended by great difficulties. These were felt very particularly by the ancient Israelites and Jews, whose most important religious feasts were reckoned with reference to harvest-time. In the course of its history, various calendars were in use in ancient Israel. Later they adopted a system which was first worked out by the Greeks or the Babylonians: from time to time an intercalary (thirteenth) month was inserted, in order to bring the beginning of the lunar year into line with the beginning of the solar year. The arrangement at present is that in a series of nineteen years, intercalary months of thirty days are inserted in the third, sixth, eighth, eleventh, fourteenth, seventeenth and nineteenth year. Smaller adjustments do the rest.

The lunar calendar, like the solar, does not allow New Year's Day to fall always on the same day of the week, any more than other feast-days. But a calendar was in use at Qumran which provided for this very thing. They divided the year into four periods of three months, in series of thirty, thirty and thirty-one days. The year was thus 364 days. As this number is divisible by seven, New Year's Day fell always on the same day of the week (apparently Wednesday, the day of the creation of sun and moon) and so too the other feast-days. The year was, however, a day short and in the long run this must have made itself felt in a disturbing manner. We do not yet know how they grappled with this difficulty; the simplest way would have been to insert an intercalary week at set times; but it is best not to speculate about the matter. Some scholars think that the calendar was in use for only a short time, so that the difficulty never became noticeable; this, however, conflicts with the great significance which the men of Qumran are known to have attributed to the calendar.

Probably the calendar of the 364-day year was no new invention but the reflection of ancient and presumably priestly traditions. It has been remarked that various precise datings in the so-called priestly parts of the Pentateuch, in the books of Chronicles-Ezra-Nehemiah, which take such an interest in everything priestly, and in the book of the priestly prophet Ezechiel, take on a new relief if one assumes that the authors of these books used this same calendar as the basis of their calculations. If this is correct, the calendar in question may have been part of the priestly tradition, which could explain the significance which was attached to it by the priestly sect of Qumran. They were convinced that it alone was correct and lawful. Those who did not celebrate their feast on the days appointed by the sect's calendar, did not fulfil the divine commandment, in the view of the sect. Hence the members of the sect repeatedly inculcated the celebration of feasts on the correct day, not too early and not too late.

We know what the calendar of feast-days meant in the East in ancient times, and what it still means. The Christians of the second century did not all celebrate Easter on the same day. Pope Victor I (A.D. 189–199) decided to put an end to that; he even went so far as to be ready to excommunicate the Christians of Asia Minor, who followed an ancient custom of celebrating the Pasch on the same day as the Jews. St Irenaeus intervened, and it seems that his action was so far successful that the excommunication was not enforced or was revoked. Even in our own day various churches in the Christian East

which claim to be orthodox still cling to the ancient Julian
Calendar; they refuse to have anything to do with the
Gregorian, which was introduced by Pope Gregory VIII in
1582. When the Gregorian Calendar (with an exception made
only for Easter) was introduced into Greece on the tenth of
March, 1924, it met with fierce opposition on the part of the
so-called palaeohemerologists, that is, the supporters of the
old way of reckoning. These regarded the imposition of a new
calendar as treason against the practice of the Fathers of the
Church, and so heresy. Even today palaeohemerologism (if
the reader will pardon the word) has not quite disappeared in
Greece, namely, at Athos. This shows us that the Qumran
community's use of a calendar different from that of the rest
of the Jews had a pronouncedly sectarian character.

That the men of Qumran placed an extraordinarily high
value on the strict observance of the dates fixed for feast-days,
can be seen from the very beginning of the Rule, where this is
presented as one of the primary duties of the members of the
brotherhood. Because after some generalities have been
uttered, we come very quickly on the following:

> All those who have voluntarily devoted themselves to the service
> of His [God's] truth must offer all their knowledge, their force
> and their possessions to the community of God; their knowledge
> shall then be brought into accord with the truth of God's laws,
> their force shall be exerted conformably to His perfect precepts,
> and their riches shall be used in accordance with His just judg-
> ment. They must in no wise depart from any precept of God for
> the time for which it is given; they must not anticipate the
> [fixed] times nor celebrate any feast on a later day; they must not
> depart from His laws to the right or to the left (Manual 1: 11–15).

One can ask oneself whether the refusal of the community to
celebrate the common Jewish feast-days at the same time as
the rest was not the most decisive reason for the formation of

the sect. No certain answer can yet be given, because it is so difficult to determine the history of the community and the motives of their conduct as long as our data are incomplete. Cleavages came about in the ancient Christian churches where differences of doctrine or religious practice were certainly not the deeper ground of schism. The causes were often political or nationalist, and were for the most part not adduced in public, being clearly insufficient to justify a cleavage in the Church of Christ. The authors of schism have for the most part tried to save their faces, with regard to themselves and the outer world, by putting doctrinal motives in the foreground, or motives borrowed from religious practices. All of which has not made it impossible for people to have worked themselves into fury at times over very minor doctrinal differences. There is therefore every reason to be still cautious in pronouncing upon the motives that led to what we must call the schism of Qumran.

It is difficult to say what other influences, besides those deriving from the religious system of Persia, affected the ways and views of the Qumran community. But of its genuinely Jewish character there is no doubt. There were no 'heresies' among them in our sense of the word, though admittedly the fact that they followed a different calendar must have meant to the rest of the Jews what heresy means to us. It is hard to tell with certainty how they came to adopt this calendar. One can only guess, and one will hardly be far out in assuming that the personal views of a group of older members, or of the Teacher himself, were of decisive influence. Some have thought that the influence of Pythagoras or Pythagorism, or neo-Pythagorism as the case may be, can be discerned among the Essenes. However, as little or nothing is certain in the matter, it is better left undiscussed.

5

THE ORGANIZATION OF THE
BROTHERHOOD

OUR chief source of information about the manner in
which the brotherhood of Qumran was organized is the
Rules which were found among the manuscripts of the
caves. The best known of these is the so-called 'Damascus
Document', fragments of which, indeed, have been found in
the Qumran caves, but of which the largest portion came to
light fifty years ago from a long-forgotten room in an old
Jewish synagogue at Cairo. It was published at Cambridge in
1910. Then there is the great Rule from Qumran, and finally
a document consisting of only two columns and hence
naturally called the 'Two-Column Document' and sometimes
'The Rule of the Congregation'; in contrast, the great Rule is
then called 'The Rule of the Community' (Hebrew: *serek ha-
yahad*). The evidence from these Rules is to be completed by
what ancient writers, especially Josephus, can tell us about the
Essenes. It is the great similarity between what the ancient
writers say, and the contents of the three Rules that makes it
clear that Essenism and the community of Qumran are
connected. None the less, when we compare Essenism and the
Rules, we come up against certain problems, because there are
some discrepancies, and even the Rules do not fully agree
with one another.

Scholars have in fact tried to work out how the various
texts and statements of Philo, Josephus, Cairo and Qumran

are related to each other, which are the older and which the later, whether they held good for all members of the sect at the same time and so forth. Some have boldly stated that the Essenes of Philo and Josephus have nothing to do with the community of Qumran. Others prefer to speak in this connexion of 'kindred groups'. It has been said that Palestine in the time of Christ was swarming with baptist sects; the community of Qumran was one of them, the sect of the Damascus Document another, the Essenes were a third, and possibly these last were again divided into different groups which were simply summed up under the name of Essenes.

Philo says that the Essenes lived a community life. They dwelt together in groups, they paid in their income to the community, they all ate of the same food at one table which was furnished from a common stock of provisions, their clothes were common property, and they kept open house for all who shared their ideals. All he says about organisation is that there was an administrator in each group who had charge of the community chest.

Josephus is much fuller, but some traits of his description are obscure. To what we already know from Philo he adds that it was the community that chose the administrator of its goods. The magistrates (=the administrators?) give precise instructions to each of the members; when they get permission, they may give aid to those who are worthy of help but without permission from the administrator, they may not even help their parents. Anyone who misbehaves may be expelled; the sentence to that effect must be passed by at least a hundred members and there is no appeal. Decisions in the assembly are taken by majority vote. The community is divided into four classes according to the length of time one has spent in it. It is not clear whether Josephus means by this the various periods of probation which precede full membership, or a division according to seniority after the period of probation. Those who present themselves for membership must first spend a full year outside the community in a sort of noviceship where they must follow the community's way of life. The successful candidate must then undergo a second period of probation. According to the most general interpretation of the text, this lasts two years, during which the candidate is admitted to more important ritual ablutions than in his first year, but not to the common table of the fully approved members. It is possible that this two-year probation was two-fold, two periods of one year each: but it is not clear. It may also be that the text intends to say that after the very first year of probation there is to be a further special period of probation, the length of which is not given, before the two-year probationary period begins. If all goes well, the candidate is admitted to full membership, which he acquires by taking a grave oath.

Each particular group had its guest-master, whose duty it was to provide from the common fund for all members who came to visit them from other parts. The advantage of this was that the members needed to take nothing with them on their travels except weapons with which to defend themselves against possible bandits. Most Essenes seem to have been unmarried, but Josephus says expressly that there were also married ones, living exactly the same life as the others, except that they were married. The unmarried Essenes adopted young children to bring them up in the sect's way of life.

If we look now at the great Rule of Qumran, we find there most of the practices and precepts which distinguish the Essenes as described by Philo and Josephus, besides a number of others. What strikes us most is the role played by the priests in the organization, about which both Philo and Josephus are silent. They, however, were writing for non-Jews, or at

least had non-Jewish readers continually in mind. Hence they
sometimes omit matter that is specifically Jewish and not of
great interest to the reader. The reason why the priests are
constantly mentioned in the scrolls and given the first place is
not far to seek: they know the Law of Moses better than any,
and they are its qualified interpreters, by virtue of ancient
prerogative. Here we must undoubtedly recall the archaic
words which Moses, according to the book of Deuteronomy,
pronounces over the members of the tribe of Levi: 'For they
have kept Thy word, they uphold Thy covenant. They teach
Jacob Thy ordinances, and Israel Thy law' (Deuteronomy
33: 9–10).

According to the prophet Aggeus (Haggai) in 520 B.C., it is
the priests who decided what is clean or unclean (Aggeus
[Haggai] 2: 11–12). A little less than a century later, Malachias
(Malachi), who closes the series of the minor prophets in the
Bible, tells us that God speaks as follows of the levitical
priesthood: 'My covenant have I made with him, life and
well-being, both have I given him, and reverence, so that he
honoured Me, and feared My name. The law of truth was in
his mouth, and evil was not found on his lips. He was ready
and upright to do My will, and he turned many away from
iniquity. For on the lips of the priest is wisdom, from his
mouth comes the instruction that men seek; for he is an envoy
from the Lord of hosts!' (Malachi 2: 5–7). At the time of
Jesus, the depositories of knowledge of the Law were above
all the scribes, who, like the later rabbis in general, were not
necessarily of priestly stock. On this point, as on so many
others, the community of Qumran was consciously more
conservative. They wanted the priests to have everything that
tradition had ascribed to them from time immemorial, in
contrast to the custom that was constantly gaining ground, of
putting competence above office. However, they also pro-

vided for experts, since the study of the Law was the primary task of the priests and of the community in general; each one took part in it according to his ability.

At the head of the sect stood 'twelve men and three priests' who must be of irreproachable conduct and also completely masters of the whole revealed Law (Manual 8: 1). Unfortunately the text does not make it clear whether the three priests formed part of the group of twelve or made a total of fifteen with it. In the former case, the college of twelve would offer a remarkable resemblance to that of the twelve apostles, among whom three were outstanding, Peter, James and John; there is, however, no indication at all that the three 'pillars' of the Church (Galatians 2: 9) also belonged to the Jewish priesthood. Possibly the resemblance, if there is one at all, is completely fortuitous.

The twelve or probably fifteen men obviously formed the ordinary council of the brotherhood. The man who is called in one place the '*mebaqqer* of the community' was probably at their head. *Mebaqqer* is a Hebrew word, an active participle of the verb *baqar*, which means to inspect, visit, supervise, investigate, exactly the same as the verb from which the Greek *episcopos* (our 'bishop') is derived. He had to provide for and supervise the community. The name indicates, to be sure, that he was to be no despot, as indeed is clear from many other passages in the Rule. Important decisions were taken in the general assembly by all those present, in so far at least as no theoretical questions were at stake, these being reserved to the priests' control. The general 'overseer' is once called '*paqid*', which means the same thing, but brings out better his authority to command. There were probably subordinate 'overseers' as well, as one would expect in a community with so many classes and functions as that of Qumran; there is express mention in one place of an 'overseer over the work of the community'.

Life in community made it necessary that each particular group should have its director. In each section, even when it numbered only ten members, a priest was to be present who was not to leave the group, and whose duty it was to study the Law continually, in order to learn ever better to know the will of God. Even today, among practising Jews, a quorum of ten males of thirteen years of age or more is necessary, and sufficient, to hold the synagogue service and perform certain religious ceremonies.

If we disregard those who were merely aspiring to membership, the brotherhood was divided into priests, levites and 'the people'. There is, indeed, also mention of 'priests, elders and the rest of the whole people', but here the levites have apparently been included among the priests and the 'elders' given special mention. These 'elders' are old or eminent men who for various reasons such as age, personal ascendancy or frequent contributions to the common counsel, form a special group in Near Eastern tribes or communities, and join the head or heads in consultation about measures to be taken, even though they have not been appointed to such an office. The sect is further divided into groups of 1,000, 100, 50 and 10. This division perhaps considers things as they ought to be rather than as they are; it goes back to a well-known element of ancient tradition. This is the way, for instance, that Moses enumerates the people of Israel, in the book of Exodus, as they were still wandering in the desert (Exodus 38: 21–25). The community of Qumran aimed at being the new Israel and therefore wanted to maintain this enumeration, which is military in origin; we cannot say how it was applied in practice or in places where there were not thousands to work with. Perhaps the names of thousands, hundreds, etc., were given symbolically to certain units, in the hope that they would be brought up to full strength when the time was ripe.

Three things are especially stressed in the Rule as community practices: the holding of common meals, praising God, taking counsel. To this was added the duty of studying the Law in common and the reading of the sacred books, which was always followed by prayer. A third part of the night was to be allotted to this by the whole community in common. The hours of the night marked out for this are not specified, so that we are reduced to hypotheses. Perhaps they began at sunset when according to Jewish reckoning the new day began; perhaps they relieved each other in three groups, so that prayer and study was kept up the whole night. The Romans divided the night into four watches, and it appears from the New Testament that this custom had been adopted in Palestine. The ancient Israelites, however, divided the night into three watches of about four hours each, and this ancient custom will have been retained at Qumran.

Each year a solemn reunion took place at which the general condition of the community was discussed and each member was assigned the place due to him at the moment. How exactly precedence was allotted is not clear. It has been suggested that each one was assigned a place in keeping with his merit and conduct, more or less the way places are distributed to children in class at the end of the school year; but whereas scholastic honours correspond mostly to success in set exams, promotion at Qumran was for virtue and diligence. There is no need to go as far as this; it is sufficient to assume that the general order of precedence was examined once more at the annual assembly and confirmed or revised as necessary. Priests took precedence over 'laymen', superiors over subjects and old people over young people. This order was to be strictly observed, as it was laid down by God; at the same time, care was to be taken that mutual harmony, charity, sincerity and uprightness were preserved.

They were to have as little as possible to do with non-members. No one was to eat or drink with them or accept a gift from them. If one needed anything from them, it was to be paid for in cash. The sharing of food and drink is taken in the Near East to the present day as a proof that people cherish peaceful intentions towards one another. Anyone who takes even a sip of coffee along with a Bedouin in the desert has nothing to fear from him as long as they are together. To refuse an offer of food and drink is therefore always taken as an insult; it may even be an expression of enmity. At Qumran, the prohibition against sharing the food of outsiders was chiefly inspired by the fear of contracting ritual uncleanness from 'unclean' food. But undoubtedly it was also a means of expressing their intention of holding themselves aloof from others as far as possible. The members of the community called themselves 'sons of light', all others were looked on as 'sons of darkness'. It is stated in the beginning of the Rule that these are to be hated, and at the end the Rule says once more that this is to be an 'eternal hatred', that is, an unconditional attitude which admits of no restrictions and of no reconsideration. St Augustine wrote in his rule that religious must have as much hatred for sin as love for the sinner; this is taken for granted in Christianity, though it is by no means easy, on account of the ineradicable inclination in all of us to equate the doer with his deeds.

At his formal reception into the community, the new member had to confess his sins in public, though in general terms only, and the sins of the whole people. The priests responded by pronouncing a blessing over the new member. Thereupon the levites cursed all the partisans of Belial, that is, all outsiders, and relegated them to 'the darkness of the eternal fire'. After that, priests and levites went on to recite together another special curse, intended for those who had perhaps joined the sect without being fully converted. Cursing and blessing have lost all or most of their meaning for modern men; but in ancient times great force was attributed to them. The ceremony of blessing and cursing at Qumran, drawn up on Old Testament lines, was meant to make a great impression on all who entered into a new 'covenant' with God, so that they would think twice about failing the obligations they had undertaken. The expression 'covenant' here signifies the bond forged with God by the taking of vows, and the duties they involve. In Christian Mesopotamia, the same expression was used for the vows which ascetics and monks made to God, who were therefore called 'sons of the covenant' in Syriac.

For the maintenance of discipline, a whole series of penalties were set down for major and minor offences. Here are some examples. For grave faults, like abusing the name of God, permanent exclusion from the community was imposed. The same penalty could be inflicted for continual bad behaviour, contrary to the spirit of the Rule. If anyone concealed his earnings or his possessions dishonestly, he was to be regarded as unclean and deprived of a quarter of his food ration for a year. The same penalty was imposed on anyone who had deliberately insulted one of the priests of the sect; if the insult was unintentional, the penalty was reduced to six months. A three months' penalty was imposed for uttering foolish, that is unseemly, talk. (It is not clear from the text what was the nature of the penalty in this and in the following cases.) In the assemblies, each one was to speak only when his turn came and no one was to interrupt another; such an interruption was penalized for ten days. Thirty days was the penalty for lying on the ground, and for going to sleep during a public session— nothing unusual in the East! The same penalty applied to spitting in the assembly. Anyone who slandered his neighbour was given a year's punishment, while anyone who brought

false accusations against the whole community was excluded
for good.

We cannot tell from the Rule whether the community consisted exclusively of men or whether women were also
admitted. Further there is no mention of celibacy. This may
be due to the incompleteness of the text; but it may also be
that the male character of the Jewish 'Brothers of the Common
Life', and the celibacy that was so closely bound up with it,
were taken so much for granted that they did not make special
mention of them. That the members called themselves 'sons'
of light may be taken as sufficient indication of it. The duties
prescribed and carried out in common are to an important
extent typically male duties in Judaism, as for instance consultation about the interests of the society, study of the Law
and prayer in common. Each male is bound to know and
study the Law; the woman is not. There were rabbis who
thought that women should be taught one or two things
about the Law, so that they could gain merit; even this was
denied by a man like Rabbi Eliezer (first century A.D.), who
said that a man who instructed his daughter in the Law was
like one who taught her lasciviousness. Hence, though it is not
expressly said, the Rule seems to imply from beginning to end
that it is drawn up for men and practised by men.

What is expressly mentioned is the obligation of bringing
all one's possessions and earnings into the community. The
practical consequences of this are hard to determine in detail.
Though the claim to personal property had to yield to the
claims of the community, the individual members must have
had certain things at their personal disposition, as is still the
case today in all monastic orders and can hardly be otherwise.
We read further that anyone who does harm to the goods of
the community must make good the damage. It is certainly
remarkable that so far none of the many caves around

8. Inside of the building near Ain Feshkha where excavations were started in 1956. This is said to be the farmhouse of the Essene settlement of Khirbet Qumran. The posts of the two doors may be seen in the corner.

9. The great assembly-hall of the main building at Khirbet Qumran. At the back are four bases, on which stood wooden columns supporting the roof. The Dead Sea is in the background (12 on plan)

10. Large cistern to the south of the main building. Two stages of the excavation are shown (17 on plan)

11. Steps leading down to cistern. The subsidence caused by the earthquake is clearly visible. Some of the plaster on the walls is still in place (17 on plan)

12. Cistern showing intake of water from conduit.

13. Room I, with plaster surrounds, the use of which is not known. Perhaps for seating, though the modern oriental finds them too narrow (4 on plan)

14. The Community Laundry (8 on plan).

Qumran has produced a single coin that can be traced to a member of the community, and that all the money that has been found was in the community building. If this means anything, it points to the fact that community of goods was strictly enforced.

The so-called 'Damascus Document' is known from two manuscripts found in Cairo, which are tenth or twelfth-century copies of the ancient texts. The first consists of eight sheets, the second of a single sheet which is nearly twice the size of any of the first. The text of the second document is to a great extent identical with that of the first half of the first, and hence the hypothesis has been put forward recently that both go back to a single original text. The first portion of the text is a lengthy admonition addressed to an organized group of pious men who have come forth from 'Aaron and Israel' and who seem at first sight identical with the sect of the great Rule. In the time-honoured Jewish fashion, selected episodes of the history of ancient Israel are put before the readers for their edification. The origin of the group is also mentioned, but the indications given are so little clear to us that very divergent explanations of them have been offered. (Some think that there is question only of the history of the group, others that it refers to the whole history of Israel.) A 'new covenant in the land of Damascus' is mentioned, but as has already been said (see above, p. 76) even this expression is interpreted in various ways by scholars. In spite of much acute analysis, no unanimity has been reached and hence it seems best to wait for new texts to be discovered, in the hope that they will cast some light on this subject.

The second part of the first manuscript, pages 9–16, is a collection of various precepts which were possibly destined for the same group as the admonition. A close inspection shows that the collection is itself built up of smaller groups of

laws which do not form a continuous whole. This was the
process which was at work in ancient times and until late in
the Middle Ages: 'codes of law' were formed from earlier
collections of customs, decrees and precepts, which were
finally put into good order by a lawgiver and then promulgated by him for a given society as 'laws' in the modern sense
of the word. When the Code of Canon Law was promulgated
in 1917, it was the first of its kind in the Catholic Church; up
to then the canonists had to deal with collections of decrees,
particular precepts, and customs with force of law and the
like, and Church law was therefore an almost unmanageable
mass of matter. On a very much smaller scale, the same was
true of the Essene communities, where there were also
various 'codes' drawn up by particular individuals. A German
scholar has proposed to call an ancient Oriental collection of
this type a 'Book of Rights' (*Rechtsbuch*) to distinguish it from
certain ancient codes and from all modern laws.

The collection contained in the Damascus Document seems
to be composed of a number of laws destined for city-dwellers,
followed by another set which envisage groups which dwell
in 'camps'. Members of the first group could possess property
in their own right, including slaves, male and female, and
could keep various other sorts of servants. They also make
offerings in the temple. The group is to have a college of ten
judges, of whom four must be of the tribe of Levi and Aaron,
the other six laymen; they are to be not less than twenty-five
and not more than sixty years old. The reason given for this
last injunction is that after sixty the mind begins to go! In the
East maturity and old age set in more quickly than with
us. It is hardly necessary to say that these judges must have a
good knowledge of the Law. They were also obliged to be
well versed in a certain book which remains a mystery to us,
called *sefer he-hagî*, which means something like 'Book of

Meditation'. It is also mentioned in the Two-Column Document. The priest, too, who is at the head of a group of ten must also read it; is it perhaps the book of the Law of Moses? The pious Israelite, according to Psalm 1, verse 2, of the biblical psalter, 'takes his delight in the Law of Yahweh, he meditates His law day and night'. This 'meditating' is much the same as studying, murmuring, reading; when the Oriental is at his sacred books, one can often see and hear the gentle murmur of his lips as he reads and studies.

Each group has also its *mebaqqer* ('overseer', 'chief'). The members must address themselves to him when they see another member committing a fault. The overseer can proceed against such an offender only when the facts are confirmed by two witnesses. A single witness is enough if the overseer has registered a first complaint in writing and the same witness catches the offender again and denounces him. It was not permissible to sell clean beasts or birds to heathens, nor the produce of threshing-floor or wine-press, or slaves of either sex who had become Jewish proselytes. It was forbidden to shed the blood of heathens for the sake of gain, nor could one seize their goods without the approval of an Israelite court. It looks very much as if these laws were intended for men who lived scattered throughout a city and not in community with one another; yet in one place a 'camp' is again mentioned. We have here a riddle which is not yet solved. Another series of rules is expressly destined for 'camps', that is, for groups of at least ten (males) who probably live in community. A priest must be present to take the decisions which the Law reserves to him; if only a weak-minded priest is available, they must still make use of him, but they must make sure that he takes his decisions in accordance with the instructions of the overseer. The latter, who is again called *mebaqqer*, is a very important man in the camp. He must teach and guide his subjects, have mercy on them like a father with his children and receive novices into the community after proper investigation. No one may be admitted without his approval, which of course does not mean that his word was enough and that the community was not also asked for its opinion.

Goods could be sold to outsiders only for cash. There is a badly preserved piece of text which may speak of the man who divorces his wife, but it is not quite clear.

The last three pages of the longer manuscript give a further set of rules for camps. There must have been a number of camps, because the text mentions the 'overseer of all the camps'. By this a single individual could be meant who stood at the head of the whole brotherhood, or the overseer of each camp. He was to be at least thirty and at most fifty years old, one who knew how to deal with men and to speak their language. He was to settle disputes among members of the community and he also decided about the admission of novices. Judges helped him to perform his duties.

The community was divided into four groups: priests, levites, Israelites (i.e. laymen) and proselytes. Proselytes were foreigners who had embraced Judaism. Each member had to pay at least two days' income each month to the overseer and the judges, who used it to establish a fund for the support of the poor, the sick, widows and orphans and other necessitous persons. There was a priest whose particular duty it was to see that the Law was kept; he is named before the overseer and must be between thirty and sixty years old. Everyone who became a member had to see to it that his sons followed him into the brotherhood when they reached the appointed age. When oaths were taken, it was forbidden to use the name of 'God' or 'the Lord', or to swear by the Law of Moses, in which the divine name occurs frequently. In uttering imprecations, one had to follow the curses written down in the Law.

The Two-Column Document, in the form in which it has reached us, is a short text containing prescriptions for 'the whole congregation of Israel at the end of days'. It is very likely that these prescriptions refer to the (ideal) future; they even envisage the possibility that the two 'Messiahs' will be present. We know on the other hand that the congregation of Qumran thought of itself as living 'in the end of days', though everything that was then to happen was far from being fulfilled.

The document begins by saying that all men, women and children must assemble to listen to the reading of the covenant and its obligations. This reminds us of the account in the book of Exodus, where we read how all Israel was gathered at the foot of Mount Sinai to listen to Moses reading the book of the covenant and promised solemnly to keep all the commandments of God. The members of the congregation are to be instructed from their youth in the Book of Meditation (i.e. the Law of Moses?) in order to know the prescriptions of the covenant; these studies are to last for ten years. At the age of twenty they are to be examined for admission to the community; the admission is decided upon by voting; at the age of twenty-five they become full members, while at the age of thirty they qualify for the most important offices. They are not to marry before they are twenty, which is very late in comparison with Jewish and Oriental usage in general. Government is in the hands of the priests and heads of families; there are also commanders of 1,000, 100, 50 and 10 men, and other officers. All these officials take part in the general councils of the whole community, over which the priests preside. The case of war is also foreseen. All counsellors and members of the community must be ritually pure; anyone who is permanently unclean from the legal point of view is to be excluded.

The order of precedence in the community is as follows: the high priest comes first, then the heads of the priestly families, each according to his dignity and office, next the anointed prince of Israel, after that the commanders of a thousand, each according to his dignity, and finally the heads of the great families and the 'sages'. This order is observed by all when they assemble; if it is for a meal, the priest first pronounces the blessing over the bread and wine that are set before him, then the 'prince of Israel' and finally all the others. These prescriptions are to be observed everywhere that ten men or more take a meal together.

It is quite clear that the Two-Column Document intends to cater chiefly for the future, but in so far as something of this future is realized in the present, its prescriptions may have had a very actual meaning.

When one compares the three Rules with one another, quite a number of differences stand out. They leave one somewhat perplexed at first and at a loss for a solution. Were collections of rules belonging to various sects and brotherhoods deposited at Qumran as though in a scientific library? It does not look like that at all, and it would be by no means in keeping with the mentality of the community. Further, it is practically certain that the Two-Column Document was sewn on to the end of the scroll containing the great Rule, so that the two formed a whole and hence were regarded as connected. For all the differences between the Rules, they have one great thing in common, their profound reverence for the Law of Moses. The lawgivers want to see this Law obeyed as precisely as is humanly possible: they prescribe that it is to be studied day and night. Now, to take one example, the Law of Moses contains many regulations with regard to matrimonial relations between man and wife, which would be meaningless if marriage was forbidden. Hence it is out of the question that the framers of the three sets of Rules regarded marriage as a prohibited institution. This holds good for the Essenes in general, as we have seen from Josephus. It follows that the practice of celibacy, which seems to be supposed by the first Rule for all who live under it, cannot have been a general law which was valid for everyone; there is no need, therefore, to be surprised when the Two-Column Document allows marriage. Since the marriage act involved ritual uncleanness for man and wife, it would have been avoided by those who desired to remain as ritually pure as possible. We should not, however, assume that the unmarried state was considered the ideal arrangement for the future era of salvation. The Two-Column Document, which, according to Gaster and others, contains the laws which will be in force in the ideal time to come, says quite the opposite and very clearly. It all fits in with what Josephus said: that there were two orders of Essenes, the married and the unmarried. The former made use of marriage only so far as was strictly necessary to beget children. This satisfied the precept of the Law which said: 'Increase and multiply.'

When we then look at the rules and customs of the Essenes against this background, it becomes conceivable that they all, in whole or in part, found their way into the one library. It had a practical end in view, the instruction and edification of the users. Hence there were several copies of each rule; in Cave 4 there were at least eleven of the great Rule and seven of the Damascus Document. The rules and the manuscripts may derive from different periods of the existence of the sect, and this may be the explanation of many of the discrepancies. It may also be that some groups went their own way, without separating from the main movement, and had some customs and practices of their own. So too in the monastic orders of the Middle Ages customs varied from abbey to abbey, though all followed the one rule. Something of the sort, though on a very small scale, was probably true of the Essene groups which were scattered here and there throughout the land. Their headquarters were set up at Qumran, apparently; here they lived as celibates under a strict community régime, and here they received also the guests who came from other parts to visit the spiritual centre. These could sleep in tents or in the caves, and when they were not ritually pure in the strict sense they did not come so easily into contact with the 'pure' members; certainly they did not eat with them at the same table.

As regards attitudes and ideals, the various groups were probably in agreement for the most part. They must all have tried to live according to the principles for ritual purity laid down by the Essenes, and probably took the organisation of the Qumran convent as a model to be reproduced as far as possible. Qumran was also their favourite burial-place; the remains of women as well as of men have been found among the skeletons that have been investigated in the cemetery, though females are so far very much in the minority. Devoted members of the sect, pious women above all, must have wished to be buried close to where so many others of outstanding piety had lived and found a last resting-place.

When one reads the text of the Rules, one must remember that they were not intended for outsiders or for the jurists of the group; they were only a sort of memorandum, booklets of rules for private use, above all for that of aspiring members. Everything was not in them, nor was everything in them equally clear. Jurisprudence was passed on from one to another chiefly by word of mouth, and hence knowledge of how rules applied was much more important than their precise formulation. When we find them differing from what Josephus and Philo tell us of the customs of the Essenes, we must remember that these two ancient writers used Greek searchlights on the life of the Essenes, so that the description they give us is coloured by being seen in an alien light. Undoubtedly Josephus and Philo give us an incomplete and partially distorted picture of the real Essenes. When this is combined with the equally incomplete picture presented by the texts of Damascus, Cairo and Qumran, we should not be surprised that we are still unable to make a detailed sketch of the movement or communities of which Qumran was the centre, or appears to have been the centre. We can only hope that texts will quickly be found and published which will throw more light on the matter.

6

THE LIBRARY IN THE CAVES

A T Qumran, men busied themselves with writing, reading
and studying. The first we know, apart from other
proofs, from the ink-wells which have been found in the
remains of the building and those of the secondary building at
Ain Feshkha, the second from the many manuscripts discovered in the neighbouring caves, the third from the prescriptions of the Rules. If all the books of which the remains
have come to light belonged to the Qumran, the community
must have possessed an extensive library, consisting of many
hundreds of volumes. But possibly members of groups which
lived outside Qumran brought their books hither in the hour
of danger, and hid them later in the surrounding caves along
with those of Qumran. As long as we have no record of what
happened here in A.D. 68 as the Roman legions, intent on
breaking all opposition, closed in on them, we can only guess.
We comprise under the name of 'the Qumran library' all that
has been found there.

The Qumran library consisted in part of biblical books, in
part of literature which was the sect's own. The books were
read intensively, and all undoubtedly served the edification
of the community. Hence the non-biblical literature must
reflect to a great extent, if not completely, the views of the
sect. In the ancient Christian Church books known to be
heretical were not read and were kept out of circulation.
Things were probably much the same at Qumran, and hence

we can use the non-biblical writings of the community to deduce with great probability the views and practices of the brotherhood. Among these are some that have been already known for a long time, such as Jubilees, Enoch and others; and it is remarkable that these are precisely the books which scholars suspected long ago to have been of Essene origin.

BIBLICAL TEXT AND BIBLICAL BOOKS

Among the biblical books, manuscripts of Deuteronomy, Isaiah and the Psalms are the most numerous. The reason is not far to seek. Deuteronomy, the fifth book of the Law of Moses, is presented as a second Law, which was proclaimed by Moses in Transjordania, at the end of the desert wanderings. It begins with a number of speeches, sermons in fact, which are placed on the lips of Moses and in which he stresses above all the special character of the people of Israel. Israel has been chosen by God from all the peoples of the world to serve Him alone. It must respond to this election by keeping the divine law and by remaining apart from all other peoples. Now the sect was convinced that it alone was the true Israel; all its members were the elect of God, and they carried this separation from all others much further than the historical Israel had ever gone. No wonder Deuteronomy was a book much read and studied at Qumran.

The biblical book of Psalms has been well called the book of Israel's piety. The community of Qumran was intensely religious and could find in the book of Psalms the best nourishment for its religious feelings. The psalms composed by the poets of the sect are to a great extent mosaics of reminiscences from the biblical psalms; their religion is a very personal matter, just as in the biblical psalms, and someone is always speaking in the first person. Hence the biblical psalms played a great part in the personal and communal life of the Qumran congregation, as they did in Christianity and Judaism. Some time ago, in 1947, I bought a roll of film at a Jewish shop in Safad in Upper Galilee. The proprietor, a small man, came forward with an old book in his hand. He showed it to me and asked me did I know it. I said yes, because it was a Hebrew edition of the Psalms, a century or two old. Then he said that he found it very beautiful and often read from it. This struck me so much that I still remember what he said: it was the expression of a religious feeling that must also have been very strong at Qumran.

The book of Isaiah is not only the most magnificent and impressive of all the prophetic books, it also contains the most extensive prophecies of a happy future. The prophets were much studied at Qumran, because the brethren were convinced that God had given the Teacher of righteousness understanding of the secret meaning of their words. Further, they were convinced that they were living in the last epoch of the dominion of evil on earth, the time of 'the reign of Belial'; they hoped it would come to a quick end, and speculated on how the end would come about. The book of Isaiah, of which one of the Fathers of the Church, St Jerome, said that it foretells the future so clearly that it could be called a fifth gospel, must therefore have held the attention of the community of Qumran in a very special manner.

All this is closely connected with three of the most important characteristics of the Qumran brotherhood: the conviction that they were the elect and therefore strictly bound to separate themselves from all that was unclean; a strongly personal religion; a life of intense expectation of the future.

As we have already said in an earlier chapter, remains of practically every book of the Hebrew Old Testament have been found in the library of Qumran, especially in Cave 4.

Only the book of Esther is still completely missing, so far, as we know. We have also said that the remains of two Hebrew manuscripts of Sirach (Ecclesiasticus), and of one Hebrew and two Aramaic texts of Tobit (Tobias) are represented among the fragments that have been found. Both of these books are regarded as deuterocanonical by Catholics, and therefore as part of Sacred Scripture, while Protestants term them apocryphal and do not count them as part of the Bible. The author of Ecclesiasticus held the high priests of his time in great honour (at the beginning of the second century B.C.), but he did not teach one of the most important elements of the doctrine of the Qumran sect, immortality in the sense of an eternally happy life in the hereafter. This could indicate that Ecclesiasticus did not find its way into the library of Qumran because of its contents, but on account of the authority which it enjoyed. As far as is yet known, no traces of other deuterocanonical books (1 and 2 Maccabees, Judith, Wisdom of Solomon and Baruch) have yet been discovered.

More important than the actual number of biblical books is the question of their text. This, however, is a matter for specialists, not for the general reader who is not at home with the many, and often very knotty problems which are presented by the study of the text and translations of the Old Testament. The autographs as they are called, that is, the copies written in their own hand by the authors of the biblical books, have all perished. What we now have are only copies. As the books were copied century after century, all sorts of mistakes have crept into the text, which should surprise nobody. There still remain some mistakes even in the printed text of a book in spite of the most careful proofreading. And the reader should see the proofs as they come from the press, when the printer is sending them to the proud —and sometimes crestfallen—author for correction! In ancient times the copying of manuscripts was a trade, with payment very often per line copied, the lines having a set or agreed average length. The more a scribe copied, the more he earned, and hence some copyists worked as fast as possible, with the result that they made many mistakes. In some cases slow and painstaking copying was combined with a careful check of the product, but the manuscripts thus reproduced were much more expensive. Further, it happened not infrequently that copyists thought themselves justified in making changes on their own initiative in the texts they were writing out, for instance, by leaving out expressions which they found strange, by adding others and modifying the text according to their own lights. The more 'sacred' a text was regarded, and thus the more inviolable, the less this was likely to occur. But when the text was considered merely as pious and edifying, the copyists could allow themselves to add something of their own to the author's original work, in order to have the result better adapted to the end in view.

There are traces of such endeavours in the library of the Qumran caves. The different copies of non-biblical texts show variants which are often much more important and extensive than those met with in the copies of biblical manuscripts. This can help us to distinguish the books that were held sacred at Qumran from those that were not, but it is of course not a criterion which can be always applied.

The Hebrew text of our printed Bibles is a sort of agreed syllabus; hence apart from tiny details, the same text is printed everywhere. This uniform text is written in the twenty-two letters of the Hebrew alphabet to which a number of signs are added: dots, strokes and tiny figures. The letters represent only the consonants, the dots, strokes, etc. the vowels and accents. These additional signs are almost entirely confined to the Bible and beginners' books. The reason is that anyone who knows Hebrew well and certainly anyone who reads, speaks or writes it daily, can get on perfectly well with the consonants alone and needs a vowel-sign only occasionally. The many vowel-signs and above all the accents make the letterpress far less restful for the eye than when it is written without these signs. The Bible, however, is read in the synagogue, and there it must be pronounced and sung exactly in all its details; hence besides the twenty-two consonants eleven other signs are used, each of which indicates some sort of vowel; the aim was to render the actual sounds as closely as possible. The sacred text was provided with a large number of 'accents', to help delivery and singing; they indicate the words that are to be joined or kept separate, and how they are to be sung. This system of accents and vowel-signs did not develop at once; in its present form it dates from the eighth century A.D. They were unknown to Qumran.

Many centuries before the complicated system of vowel-signs and accents that we know had come into use, a simpler means had been discovered for indicating at least some of the important vowels. The pronunciation of *w* and *y* in Hebrew was such that they were partly audible as the vowels *u* and *i*. Hence people proceeded to use them as vowels, first at the end of words which ended in these vowels, then also in the middle of words. Finally the *w* was also used as a long *o*, the *i* as a long *e*, while the *h* was often used to indicate a long *a* at the end of a word. The same letters *w*, *i* and *h* were, of course, still used as consonants, so that the reader had to know their value in each word. This system, which occurs also in other Semitic languages and is used there successfully, as for instance in Arabic, may strike the reader who knows no Hebrew as complicated and burdensome. If so, he forgets perhaps that in his own language vowel-signs may be used also as consonants and more important still, that the same letters may be used for very different vowels and consonants. The vowel *o* has a different value in 'pot', 'school' and 'book', while there are other variations in 'son', 'note' and 'lord'. When one thinks of the various sounds of 'bough', 'cough' and 'though', one has proof enough that the spelling of English presents problems of its own, of which those brought up on English are hardly conscious. The reason is that we do not keep pictures of letters in our imagination, but only images of words and phrases, so that we do not pay any particular attention to the letters as such. The letter-signs *i*, *w* and *h* change the picture of the Hebrew word and make it easier to read when they are put in at the right place (in any case at the end of a word ending in a vowel). Hence the Jewish grammarians, using a native idiom, called them 'mothers of reading', *matres lectionis*.

These 'mothers of reading' came into use in Hebrew from the ninth century B.C. on, while in the closely related Phoenician they were almost totally ignored. The use of them in the middle of words was limited, and had no fixed rules; each one could write them or leave them out. After the exile, however, they came to be written more and more; this development was carried furthest in a number of manuscripts of the Qumran library: in a number of biblical and in many non-biblical texts. There was no unified system of spelling in the community of Qumran, so that spelling was one more of their problems.

Among the biblical manuscripts, we find some which are provided with a large number of these *matres lectionis*, far more than in the printed text of the Hebrew Bible nowadays, and others that were more sparing in their use, and which agree on this point more or less with our printed text. This is to be explained by assuming that the old traditional way of writing was kept in a number of manuscripts, while a more popular way of writing Hebrew was used in others. This latter feature enables us to determine that Hebrew was not pronounced at Qumran in the same way as it is today. This, however, is not a new discovery. Anyone who notices how proper names from the Old Testament are spelt in the Greek and Latin texts and their translations, will find a remarkable difference which extends over the whole list when he compares the spelling of the Hebrew and of translations from it. The same king of Babylon who appears in some texts as Nebuchadnezzar or Nebuchadrezzar is called Nabuchodonosor by others, following the way of writing the name in the ancient Greek version, which was taken over by the Latin. How did the difference come about? In the original Babylonian the king in question was called Nabu-kudurri-usur. The name was debased in popular usage to Nabuchodonosor and Nebuchadrezzar, and the former of these two pronunciations, which is found in the Greek and Latin texts, is clearly closer to the authentic than the latter. This is only one example from many. So we should not be at all surprised that Hebrew was not pronounced at Qumran in exactly the same way as it was pronounced eight to ten centuries later by the Lake of Tiberias, where the pronunciation in use today was fixed.

More important than differences of spelling are differences in the actual text of the Bible. The reader who is not an expert in the comparative study of biblical texts and their ancient versions should not make too much of it. For the specialist in textual criticism, the differences he notes between the text of the Qumran Bible and that of the modern Hebrew Bible are often of great scientific interest; for the general reader who uses the Bible in a modern translation for his own instruction and edification, they are in general of no great significance. The most important differences are as a rule no greater than those which ordinarily distinguish the Septuagint from the current Hebrew text. In expressing ourselves in this manner, we are consciously adopting the point of view of the modern reader. The ancient Church took a different view of variations in the text. When St Jerome at the end of the fourth century and the beginning of the fifth made an independent translation of the Old Testament from the Hebrew, the resulting Latin version threw the Church into a tumult. The learned Father was blamed for producing a version which departed from the Septuagint and the Old Latin translation which was based on it, and so from the Church Bible. The ordinary faithful and part of the clergy were very devoted to the letter of their biblical text, and took all departures from it very ill. Good sense finally triumphed and St Jerome's version, now known as the Vulgate, completely eliminated the older text. The Vulgate was better than the Old Latin version, and dogma was not endangered.

No uniform text of the Bible, fixed in all details, existed at the time of the community of Qumran. The many manuscripts of the Bible showed variations one from another, and they were left in that state. The commentaries give us to understand that two different readings of the same text were allowed the same value. Old Mohammedan writers did the same thing with variant readings of the Koran. After the fall of the temple of Jerusalem, the Jews decided to bring about complete uniformity in the text of the Bible, as a further expression of the unity of Judaism. This probably took place at the synod which the rabbis held at Jamnia in Palestine towards the end of the first century. They went back to the text that seemed to offer most guarantees of age and authenticity. This text is already represented in the writings of Qumran, though it is not the only one there. It is also relatively the best, though this judgment is true only of the text as a whole, and not of all details. And the textual problem is not the same for each book of the Bible.

Here are some examples which may give the reader an idea

of the matter in question. The great Isaiah scroll, found in Cave 1, shows twenty-three departures from the ordinary Hebrew text in the famous Chapter 53 which tells of the Man of Sorrows. A number of these variants have to do with spelling, in others the word 'and' is added without changing the meaning, in others again a word is read somewhat differently, without affecting the sense of the phrase in which it occurs. Only three variants are of some importance. In verse 9 we read: 'with the rich is his tomb' instead of 'with the rich among his dead'; in verse 10: 'he pierced him' instead of 'he made [him] ill'; in verse 11: 'out of [after] the misery of his soul he shall see *light*, he shall be sated' instead of 'out of [after] the misery of his soul, he shall see, be sated'. From the point of view of textual criticism these variants, the last of which was already known from the Greek, have their importance. They do not alter the meaning of the chapter, and its interpretation (which is very much disputed) does not need to be modified one way or the other. In the thirty-one verses of Chapter 1 of the same book there are twenty-five variants; the most important of them is in verse 15, because at the end of this verse we read not only 'your hands are full of blood' but an additional 'your fingers full of iniquity'. The other variants are again differences of spelling, insertion of a conjunction or possessive pronoun (without change in the meaning of the text) and so on. They interest specialists, who can draw conclusions from them about the transmission of the text. The chief conclusion is that the Isaiah text in the great scroll has a very long history behind it, during which it was touched up here and there, principally to make it more readable. Some of the variants perhaps reproduce a more original text, in the majority of cases they do not.

We have used here the great Isaiah scroll as a sample, because it is the one which contains most variants. Other

texts so far published offer far fewer. An exception must be
made for some fragments from the book of Samuel which
were published three years ago by Frank M. Cross. Specialists
in textual criticism had already known for a long time that the
Hebrew and the Greek texts of the book of Samuel displayed
'notable' differences. Some of these differences were explained
by the supposition that the Greek translator had a somewhat
different text before him than we now possess. Opinions
differed about other variants. Some were inclined to hold the
Greek translator chiefly responsible for them, on the grounds
that he allowed himself extensive liberties; others preferred to
think of another Hebrew text as the basis of the translation.
The publication of the fragments of Samuel mentioned above
which date from the first century B.C. has made the latter
hypothesis likely. The variants in the Hebrew text now
published appear in fact to agree with the Septuagint against
the ordinary text.

The conclusion to be drawn from this is that the text of
Samuel was not uniformly transmitted over a period, but was
copied with a great number of variants in the manuscripts.
Out of the current texts and perhaps variants also a choice was
finally made. The mutual discrepancies are too great to be
explained by slips of the pen and the normal small liberties
which copyists usually allow themselves. It is now clearer
than before that over a certain period the text of the book of
Samuel was pretty freely handled. We know that that also
happened with the text of a book like Tobit (Tobias) because
mutually divergent texts or translations of it are still known
in their entirety. The handiest explanation is that there was a
period during which the book of Samuel, like Tobias, was not
regarded by everyone as sacred and canonical and therefore
unalterable. To suit their taste or to embroider the text,
copyists added paragraphs here and there when transcribing

the book, left out others and made small changes. It is also clear that they were sometimes not careful enough with their work; thus in the current Hebrew text of Samuel slovenliness alone is responsible for the omission of whole lines which are still to be found translated in the Greek text.

Fragments like those of Samuel give us an opportunity of seeing the actual processes which were at work while the text of the book was becoming increasingly uniform. The modern reader should not forget that a book was 'ownerless' in ancient times, and that there was no copyright. When a copyist thought that a text that he was transcribing could be 'improved' or embellished by additions, omissions or modifications, he did not leave it unaltered. Not so long ago it was the custom among the Atyehs of Sumatra that a copyist *had* to give proof of his good taste by embellishing the text of a saga that he was transcribing; the custom was noted by Snouck-Hurgronje at the end of the last century, and Atyeh is no exception to the rule. As soon, however, as one is convinced that a text is sacred, or is in the nature of revelation, one tries to transmit it exactly and without alteration. Further, one must not exaggerate the difference of text in the transmission of the book of Samuel; it does not affect the essential uniformity. No new Bible is being discovered at Qumran.

Finally, some *Greek* biblical texts have been found at Qumran, which may perhaps throw new light on the question of the origins of the famous Greek version of the Bible. According to the well-known account given by an anonymous Jew who wrote under the name of Aristeas, King Ptolemy II of Egypt (285–246 B.C.) sent for seventy-two scholars from Jerusalem, six from each tribe, who worked together for seventy-two days and translated the whole Law of Moses from Hebrew into Greek. Probably the only true part of this story is that the Law was translated into Greek in

Egypt some time in the third century B.C. In the imagination of Jews and Christians it later took a form which it had not at first. The legend was that the seventy-two men had translated the whole of the Old Testament into Greek. On the island of Pharos in the Mediterranean, off Alexandria, they had been shut away in seventy-two different cells where they accomplished the work under the inspiration of the Holy Ghost. When they were finished, lo and behold, they had all translated the whole text in exactly the same way! In the time of St Jerome a guide was still showing the cells to the tourists visiting Pharos. As a result of this legend, the translation received the name of the Septuagint, that is, the Seventy (really seventy-two) men.

The facts are quite different. A long time passed, perhaps as much as a century and a half or more, before the translation of all the books of the Bible into Greek was completed. The work was certainly not performed by a permanent committee of translators; very much of it is due to the initiative of individuals. The value of the work is therefore unequal in parts; the translation is good in some books, less good in others, and in some definitely bad—at least according to our standards. The translator of the very difficult book of Job took the liberty of abbreviating his text to an important extent. Like every translation, the Septuagint is frequently in the nature of a commentary; sometimes it paraphrases, at times it clarifies the text to some extent or replaces offensive words by others. Here, therefore, the Italian proverb may frequently be applied: *traduttore traditore*: 'the translator is a traitor'; he betrays the text by not rendering it properly, he betrays himself by putting down his own thoughts in the translation. Hence the Septuagint is an important source of our knowledge of the views of Greek-speaking Jews of the last centuries before our era, a source that as yet has been only partially tapped.

From many points of view, the Septuagint is no unified text-form. Not only does the value of the translation vary widely from book to book, but the text has been constantly revised in the course of centuries and thus did not remain unaltered. No single uniform text ever took shape out of the revisions, but different, mutually divergent texts remained side by side and were used side by side. The great ancient manuscripts of the Septuagint, which are all of Christian origin, diverge from one another in their text. At present many scholars hold that this diversity is not sufficiently explained by the various modifications which a single text underwent in the course of time. They think that this diversity is not the result of evolution from an original unity, but that it was there from the beginning: in other words, that the different and mutually divergent forms in which the text of a single book appears can be due, and is actually due to the fact that different translations were originally made of the same book. Furthermore, the word 'translation' should in most cases be taken with a grain of salt, because we are often dealing with explanations and paraphrases of the text, in the nature of the Jewish *targums*, which are also interpretation rather than translation, as the term implies.

It is difficult to form a personal opinion about the problem of the origin and nature of the Septuagint. The views of great scholars are very much opposed to each other on this point; one of the reasons which make such conflicting views possible is the fact that we know so little of the early history of the Septuagint, above all of its history while still in the hands of the Jews. We know something of it from the martyr St Justin (died 165). In his dialogue with Tryphon (possibly the famous rabbi Tarphon) he says that the Jews of his day read a number of texts of the Septuagint quite differently from the Christians, the reason being that they had altered these texts in their own Greek Bibles. St Justin adduces a number of examples from this modified Jewish Septuagint translation. The work of St Justin is known to us only from a single manuscript of the fourteenth century, and a very poor one at that, so it must be approached very cautiously. That is what was in fact done, and scholars were even so cautious that they gave no credence to the authenticity of the Greek texts adduced by St Justin; at any rate they were known from no other source.

A change has now come over this situation, since the desert of Judah yielded some remains of a Greek scroll of the minor prophets where the text is in entire agreement with the Greek translation described by St Justin. The manuscript, written throughout in fine, even, Greek capitals (uncials), is from the end of the first century A.D. This important discovery reminds us of how little we know about the early history of the Septuagint and how careful we must be in proposing theories about it. This is something with which not only scholars are concerned; the reader of the Bible can also be affected by it, without knowing it. It has in fact long been the custom when translating from the Hebrew text into a modern language, to take into account the Septuagint and other ancient versions. In places where the Hebrew text is unintelligible, or appears to be, and the Septuagint gives a good meaning, it is tempting to alter the Hebrew according to the Septuagint, which is often called, without further ado, 'correcting' it. The translation of the Old Testament now being produced by the Catholic Biblical Association of America provides examples of this procedure which are discussed in the notes. To be able to correct the Hebrew according to the Greek it is first and foremost necessary to know the value, the significance, the history and the original text of the Septuagint. We must know what the Septuagint is worth. The study of this has still advanced only a short distance. Finds like those of the desert of Judah help the scholars further.

Besides biblical texts, many more non-biblical texts have been discovered. A number of these have already been cited and used in preceding chapters. Here we give a list of them with a description of them and a short summary of their contents.

BIBLE COMMENTARIES

According to the views of the sect, the Teacher of righteousness was enlightened by God 'to know all the secrets of the prophets'. Possibly he was not the only one to feel himself inspired in this way. In any case the words of the prophets were 'explained' at Qumran in a way that makes us think of the expression just quoted. The remains that have been found of biblical commentaries all belong in fact to the same type, one which had hitherto been completely unknown. They quote and explain the text of the prophets or the psalms verse by verse. The explanation is given the name of *pesher*, a word that is used indeed in the Old Testament for the interpretation of dreams. Daniel is enlightened beforehand by the spirit of God, so that he can explain the dreams of Nabuchodonosor, which none of his sages can interpret. We cannot but think of this when we observe the manner in which prophets and psalms are explained at Qumran; a meaning is given to the texts which no one who did not know it would suspect to be in them. What the prophets say is referred, not to the time and the events which they obviously intend, but to the time of the writer and the history of the sect. For example:

'Therefore he sacrifices to his net, and burns incense to his dragnet' (Habacuc 1: 16): the meaning is that they offer sacrifice to their standards and do reverence to their weapons of war. 'For thereby he gathers rich booty and his food is luxurious' (Habacuc 1: 16):

the meaning is that they divide their yoke and their forced labour of which they enjoy the fruits, over all peoples year by year, so that they lay waste many lands. 'Therefore he draws the sword unceasingly while he slays peoples and spares none' (Habacuc 1: 17): this means the Kittim who put to death many by the sword, youths, men and greybeards, women and children; even on the unborn child they have no mercy.' (Habacuc Commentary 6: 2–12.)

Habacuc, who lived in the seventh century B.C., was speaking of the Chaldaeans whose speedy arrival in Judaea he foretold. The commentator, who lived probably in the first century B.C., read into the text a meaning which made it refer to the enemies of his own day, the 'Kittim', here presumably the Romans, in any case enemies of Israel living in the second or first century B.C. This is foreign to the text of Habacuc, but the commentator puts it into it; his 'exposition' should therefore rather be called an imposition of his own meaning upon the text. How far he can go can be seen from the following example from the same commentary:

'On account of bloodshed, and violence done to the land, the city and all who dwell therein' (Habacuc 2: 8): this means the wicked priest, who for the crime he committed against the teacher of righteousness and his fellows was delivered by God to his enemies, that they might humble him and deal him a destructive blow, which he shall feel bitterly, because he did evil against His chosen ones (9: 9–12).

The text quoted from Habacuc (see Habacuc 2: 8) says nothing at all of priest or teacher, who are contemporaries of the commentator; the author simply invents the reference and imports it into the text.

Now one may ask oneself how far the authors of such commentaries regarded their interpretation as a genuine sense of the text, something it really meant, though perhaps mysteriously. Did they perhaps only intend to *accommodate* the words of the prophets to the circumstances of their own day, just as Jesus sometimes did (compare St Matthew 15: 7–9) and as is done with texts from the Bible even in our own day? The answer must be that we do not yet know enough about these *pesher*-commentaries to give an answer that excludes all doubt. The most obvious solution is that the writers thought that God had put words on the lips of His prophets which contained besides their ordinary meaning a hidden significance, known to the sect by divine revelation. This revelation may have been given in general terms, so that the members of the sect had themselves to find the meaning of this or that particular text, once the guiding lines were laid down. The principle then was: all the words of the prophets have a special significance for our day; this period is 'the last days', now comes the great decision which will settle for good the lot of mankind; God comes to judge the world, to condemn the wicked and reward the good for ever by setting up a kingdom for them; God had all this in mind when He sent His prophets and caused them to speak about it in mysterious prophetic language, which they did not themselves fully understand. When this principle is applied to the interpretation of a text, the text is readily *accommodated* to the events of the commentator's day. This is what happened at Qumran and hence their biblical commentaries display a mixed character where the dividing-line between explanation of the text and adaptation by the commentator is very fluid. One is probably right in adding here that the primary intention of the commentator was not scientific exegesis which would give the meaning of the text in a solid and impeccably correct way; he was writing edifying literature in which the events of his day would appear in the light of revelation, which had, of course, a bearing on his own day. There is plenty of room for imagination in this procedure.

It is difficult to reproduce in brief the contents of the Habacuc Commentary. It deals only with the first two chapters of this small book, omitting the third. This last is a psalm which described a theophany, that is, a divine manifestation, in poetic fashion, and which therefore deals with quite a different subject from Chapters 1 and 2. In Chapter 1, Habacuc describes the coming of the fierce Chaldaeans, in Chapter 2 he foretells their punishment. The commentator applies the first part to the coming of the Kittim, whom nobody and nothing can escape, i.e., the Romans, or enemies of Israel in general; the second part is referred to the punishment which the wicked priest and his followers must undergo for their criminal behaviour towards the Teacher of righteousness. What precise crime they committed is not said; some modern commentators think of murder, but that is not in the text. Still less is there any suggestion that the disciples of the Teacher awaited his resurrection and his second coming to judgment. The Teacher is also no Messiah, no anointed redeemer, in fact no prophet like his predecessors, but simply an inspired interpreter of the prophets. The wicked priest was looked on as faithful in the beginning, but that did not last long. His priests committed robbery and enriched themselves in an unjust manner. On a great Day of Expiation, the Priest appeared in the house where the Teacher and his followers were living in exile. He intended to handle them with violence, or he actually did attack them (the text is not sufficiently clear) and tried to make them desecrate their holy day.

Efforts have been made to identify the Wicked Priest and the Teacher with persons known to history, but hitherto no one has succeeded in doing so. There are even scholars who aver that the titles 'Teacher' and 'Priest' do not refer to two definite persons, but to a whole series. T. Gaster has even maintained that 'the Teacher' means every teacher of Israel and of the sect, past and present. Certainty is not yet arrived at on this point. The present writer has always had the strong impression that we are dealing with only two individuals, and this opinion is shared by the vast majority of commentators. The 'Biblical Commentaries' vibrate with impassioned feeling, the Wicked Priest is the object of loathing, contempt and horror, his punishment by God is foretold. This gives the impression that the Wicked Priest is a very definite person. He persecuted and abused the Teacher, and this is spoken of with so much vehemence that here again it is difficult to envisage more than one person for the role.

The identification of the Teacher is up to the present completely unsuccessful, though a legion of names have been mentioned. The possibility of identifying the Wicked Priest looks somewhat better, because everything points to the fact that he was a high priest of the time of the Maccabees or Hasmonaeans (see p. 59 above). But even here one is groping in the dark, because there are many candidates, and the historical background of the Habacuc Commentary is still far from clear. The publication in 1956 of fragments of a Nahum Commentary cast light on the subject, according to some. The names of historical personages are given for the first time in this commentary: Demetrius and Antiochus, along with the 'rulers of the Kittim' and the 'kings of Greece'. Antiochus is Antiochus Ephiphanes and the Kittim are the Romans; Demetrius is probably Demetrius III who round about 88 B.C. came into conflict with Alexander Jannaeus, as has been described already (see p. 60 above).

If the 'ravening lion' is the same as the 'wicked priest', the latter must be Alexander Jannaeus: but this cannot yet be proved. The question remains open.

All that is left of commentaries on Isaiah, Micah (Micheas), Zephaniah (Sophonias), Hosea (Osee) and the Psalms consists of small pieces only. The commentaries on Micheas and Psalm 37 mention the Teacher and his opponent.

RULES

Besides the Commentaries, a number of Rules have been found, of which we have spoken in the previous chapter when describing the organization of the sect. We add here some details.

The great Rule was called 'The Manual of Discipline' by its editor, Millar Burrows, and it is still known by this name in many publications. Later it was proposed to call it 'The Rule of the Community', which renders the Hebrew *serek ha-yahad*. The Hebrew name is undoubtedly the best and the most characteristic, but a good translation of it is difficult. The text of the Rule does not give the impression that it is all of one piece; Burrows had already suggested that it is composed of elements of diverse origin. It consists of eleven columns, with twenty-six lines to the column, and has been preserved practically in its entirety.

The text begins with a general introduction which urges the necessity of keeping the Law of Moses, of doing good and avoiding evil, of loving the sons of light and hating the sons of darkness. Anyone who wishes to become a member of the community must bind himself by a grave oath, called 'covenant', to keep the customs of the community. Each year there is a solemn reunion where the covenant is renewed and blessing and curse pronounced. Then comes the famous passage, a column and a half long, about the 'two spirits' of light and darkness, of good and evil, which try to bring men to follow the promptings of each. After that follow regulations about the order in the community; the priests have precedence and control; the members must be ritually pure and abstain from all that is unclean; the behaviour and intentions of the would-be members are to be carefully examined. Then come various regulations, dealing, for instance, with the obedience due to superiors, meals in common, the study of the Law, the manner of assembling, and so on. A whole column is devoted to a list of offences and their punishments; it is obviously only a selection from all that might have been said. The chief crimes mentioned are: dishonesty with regard to community property; abuse of the name of God; disobedience; bringing false charges against a fellow member or quarrelling with him; bad language; misbehaviour during assembly; apostasy or an equivalent attitude. Clearly, the rule names only offences which affect the community life as such, including for instance swearing, which was forbidden to Essenes. The heaviest punishment was definitive exclusion from the community; lighter penalties which could easily be incurred were temporary banishment from the group of the 'pure' and the withholding of part of the food ration. A number of considerations, some of a pious nature, interspersed with various precepts, and a concluding psalm, terminate the Rule. The final psalm belongs to the Rule: it includes, for instance, a summary of various duties of their state in life for members of the sect.

The composition of this Rule is not completely unique or extraordinary. The book of Ecclesiasticus, which purports to be a rule of life for the pious Israelite who keeps the Law of Moses, begins with general considerations and closes with two psalms. From Greek antiquity, the statutes of a religious association of Bacchus-worshippers, the so-called Io-Bacchi, have been preserved; the statutes, from the second century A.D., regulate the following cases: admission of members;

times of assembly; penalties and fines; the ceremonial of assembly, where for instance an address was given; celebration of special occasions in the lives of members; rights and duties of the treasurer; duties of the members at the funeral of one of their fellows. It is noticeable that the Rule of Qumran caters to some extent for the same situations as that of the Io-Bacchi, some elements coming in practically the same order in both. They have, of course, no connexion with each other, but the resemblances they display indicate well enough that certain forms of community life were flourishing in the Hellenistic world in the centuries round the beginning of our era, and that they showed similar features even in different places and in very different settings. Ever since Josephus, the likeness between the Essene brotherhood and that of the Pythagoreans or neo-Pythagoreans has been noted. The organization of these latter is, however, not well known, while the statutes of the Io-Bacchi are the only ones of the type preserved from antiquity.

We have already spoken at length of the Damascus Document, or the Damascus Rule, in the previous chapter.

THE WAR RULE

Quite another piece of writing is the War Rule, originally called *The War of the Sons of Light with the Sons of Darkness*. This document has reached us in a very much damaged state; we have the remains of nineteen columns and a number of fragments, most of which are very small. The bottom portion of each column has been eaten away; of the twenty-one or twenty-two lines which each column must have contained, only fourteen have remained more or less sound, in Columns 1 to 13, while in the other lines only some words have been preserved. Columns 14 to 19 are also damaged at the edges and in the middle. We have therefore less than two-thirds of the original manuscript, or perhaps even less than half. The fact that there are large gaps between the columns makes it difficult to follow the text as a whole. However, we must be grateful for the large portion that has been spared. The scroll comes from Cave 1; fragments of other manuscripts of the same text have been found in other caves, but are not yet published.

The Rule opens with the declaration that the sons of light must attack the sons of darkness. These latter are further defined as 'the army of Belial, the inhabitants of Philistia, the bands of the Kittim of Assur and of their helpers, the traitors against the covenant'. They are opposed by 'the sons of Levi, the sons of Judah, the sons of Benjamin, the exiles of the desert'. Then there will be a war between Egypt and Syria, which will put an end to Syrian rule and put the sons of light in possession of Jerusalem and the temple. There they immediately make ready for a war which will last for forty years, to be directed against the descendants of Shem, Ham and Japheth; that is, against all the peoples of the world. For six years, they take the field year by year against a different nation, but in the seventh year, in accordance with the Law of Moses, no war is waged. Once the sabbatical year is over, the campaigns are resumed. After forty years all the sons of darkness are destroyed for good.

The text describes the weapons which will be carried: shields, spears, swords, bows and slings, richly decorated with gold, silver and precious stones; the army is divided into a great many brigades and battalions, each of which fights under a banner of its own, with a motto on it as militant as it is religious. The deployment of the troops and the tactics of battle are described in detail, but all the many technical terms which are used in the account are no longer clear to us. The

fact that the text has suffered greatly also makes it impossible
for us to form a clear picture of the operations in detail.
Yigael Yadin, who was in 1948 Chief of Staff of the Jewish
armies which conquered part of Palestine from the Arabs, and
who apart from being a military man is also an expert in
antiquities, thinks that the battle tactics, as described in the
War Rule, are copied from the Romans. The priests play a
leading role in the war: just as in time of peace they are the
rulers of the people, so too in time of war they have charge of
military operations. The reason for this is to be sought
exclusively in the sacred character of the priests, not in their
greater competence or the dominant position that they hold.
The community of Qumran is directed theocratically by the
priests, in time of peace as in war. The Rule includes, further,
the text of prayers and addresses to be pronounced by the
priests before battle, and of thanksgiving hymns to be chanted
after victory.

One can see that the War Rule is a remarkable piece of
writing in which fantasy and reality are mingled. It is not an
'apocalypse', as it has been sometimes called, because an
apocalypse is a work which recounts history in the form of
secret revelations. The Rule has in view nothing more or less
than a holy war against the world, to the greater honour and
glory of the God of Israel, where the sons of light are always
the aggressors. The prophets, to be sure, knew of a violent war
in which at the end of time Israel must *defend* itself against Gog
from the land of Magog and his allied princes; they did not
foresee a holy war of aggression. The thought of an offensive
war must surely be connected with the dualism of Qumran,
in which world history as a whole was pictured as a great
battle between light and darkness, where both parties are on
the offensive. Thinking this out to its logical conclusion, they
came to the idea that the little group of the sons of light had a

vocation to attack and destroy the sons of darkness. That such was their purpose may be seen from the commentary on Psalm 37: 10, which runs: '"Yet a short while, and the wicked are no more; I look for them, but they are no more": this refers to all the wicked, who are to be destroyed in the space of forty years; then there shall be no wicked found on earth' (Fragment, column 1: 5–8).

THANKSGIVING PSALMS

We come now to a very important work, the Thanksgiving Psalms or Hymns, called *Hodayot* by their first editor, who used a Hebrew word meaning 'thanksgivings', after the opening words of many of these psalms. The manuscript, which was found in Cave 1, comprises eighteen large columns and a number of fragments, mostly very small. The columns have been badly damaged at top and bottom, and for the most part in the middle also; it is generally accepted that each column once contained forty lines or more. It was not till the end of 1954 that the complete text, in so far as it is extant, was published, at Jerusalem; the poor condition of the text is the reason why scholars offer translations of it only with hesitation. Such publications are also rendered more difficult by the fact that custom demands of the translator that he give proof of his competence and erudition by filling in the gaps in the text as far as possible and then reproducing his efforts in translation. There are very large lacunae in the text of the Hymns, and it is frequently impossible to restore them. Further, a number of fragments still remain unpublished, because they came into hands other than those of the editors of the text of Cave 1; the result of which is that any complete translation of the text of 1954 must be provisional, especially if the translator is compelled to try to fill in the gaps by conjectural restoration of the lost matter. We cannot say how many hymns have been preserved in whole or in part, because style and contents are uniform throughout, and the damaged text often does not show where one ended and another began. T. Gaster, the first translator of the hymn-book, counts nineteen in the first twelve columns of text; he did not number the rest, as they were in too fragmentary a state.

Though in many places the Hymns look like tapestries of biblical quotations, they still have a character all their own. A number of them begin with the words: 'I praise Thee, O Lord, because . . .' as does the first of the two hymns which close the book of Ecclesiasticus:

> I praise Thee, Yahweh, O King,
> I praise Thee, O God, who art my salvation!
> I shall tell of Thee, O refuge of my life,
> for Thou hast rescued my soul from death,
> Thou hast preserved my body from the grave,
> and rescued my foot from the grasp of the underworld
>   (Ecclesiasticus 51: 1–2).

Compare this with the following hymn:

> I praise Thee, O Lord,
> for Thou hast rescued my soul from the grave
> and from the corruption of Hades Thou hast brought me up
> to an eternal height (Column 3: 19–20).

The style of the Hymns is not that of the Old Testament psalms, in spite of frequent citations from them. The verses are long, sometimes very long, and remind us now and then of prose periods. It is very questionable whether they were chanted or delivered in the same way as the biblical psalms, or were rather intended for reading.

It is held by many that the Teacher of righteousness was the author of the Hymns, because some expressions which occur in them would be more intelligible on that supposition. Others oppose this view. The author of the Hymns (we omit consideration of whether there were more authors than one) thanks God for having saved him from the dangers which threatened him from his enemies. God helps him and prepares a place for him among His holy angels. God has poured out His spirit over the psalmist, who has proclaimed to others the revelations he has received and thereby become for them a support and a light. Of himself man is nothing but a sinful being; all the good that is in him has come from God, who guides his steps. It is God also who triumphs over his enemies and judges and punishes them. To give the reader an impression of the Thanksgiving Psalms, we give here in translation a hymn which has been preserved almost in its entirety:

I praise Thee, O Lord,
because Thou hast not abandoned me,
while I dwelt as a stranger among strangers. . . .
Thou hast not judged me according to my guilt,
Thou hast not abandoned me in spite of my evil thoughts,
And Thou hast guarded my life from the pit. . . .
Thou hast placed my soul amid lions
who lie in wait for the wicked,
lions who crush the bones of the mighty,
and lap the blood of the strong.
Thou hast brought me into the house of many fishermen,
who cast their net upon the waters
and pursue the doers of wickedness.
There hast Thou set me down to be judged,
but Thou hast set truth in the depths of my heart,
water of the covenant for all that seek it.
Thou hast shut the mouth of the lions
whose teeth are like daggers
and whose fangs are like sharp spears;
all whose thoughts, bent on ravage, are the venom of dragons.

Many though they be,
they do not open their jaws to devour me,
because Thou my God keepest me hidden from men,
till the moment that Thou revealest to me Thy salvation.
Because in the anguish of my soul Thou hast not abandoned me,
when I cried aloud for bitterness of soul Thou didst hear me,
and didst regard my cup of sorrows as I wept,
and Thou hast freed the soul of the poor man from the lions' den,
that sharpen their tongues like daggers.
But Thou, my God, hast stopped their mouths,
that they may not rend the soul of the poor and miserable;
Thou hast muzzled their tongue like a sword in the sheath,
that it may not strike the soul of Thy servant.
To show in me Thy might to all men,
Thou hast wrought marvellously with the poor man,
and put him like gold into the melting-pot
into the crucible of fire,
like silver to be purified in the furnace of the smith,
to refine it sevenfold.
Strong and evil men strive hard to overwhelm me,
but Thou, O God, shalt still the storm,
Thou savest the soul of the poor . . . from the might of the lions
        (Thanksgiving Psalms 5: 5–19).

Where 'soul' occurs in this text, it means life, the inward man
or man as a living being, as also in the Old Testament psalms.

Besides the Book of Hymns, remains of other poetical works
have been found, but little of them has been published.

MIDRASH ON GENESIS

Among the finds in Cave 1 was a scroll of which the
sheets were so badly stuck together that years passed before
the text it contained was known. Because the name of Lamech
occurred on a fragment that had broken off, some thought at
first that a lost apocryphal book of Lamech had been found,

known hitherto only by name. The language of the scroll was Aramaic. When the book was sold to the Israeli by the Syrian bishop and arrived in Jerusalem, they recognized that so much of the leather was not only stuck together, but was in such perishable condition that there was no further hope of reading the text on the parts in question. They separated, then, all they could from the scroll, salvaging thus the four innermost columns entire and a number of others in part, which could then be rendered legible. On 8 November 1956 Professor Maisler, president of the Hebrew University, was able to show journalists the edition of five columns of text and its translation. The text, it was clear, was not from the lost book of Lamech, but comprised copious edifying narrative about persons and events of the book of Genesis, written in the style of the *midrash*, which is a type of ancient Jewish literature, where among other things pious fiction is found. The author took as his basis the text of the biblical book of Genesis, and expanded it largely with the help of his imagination. One reads, for instance, in Genesis, Chapter 12, that the Pharaoh of Egypt fell in love with Sarah the wife of Abraham, and took her into his harem; this brought him such bad luck that he sent her back again to her lawful husband. What the ordinary Hebrew Bible takes seven and a half lines to say is expanded in the Aramaic to more than thirty lines. Genesis 12: 15 says that Pharaoh's courtiers saw the beauty of Sarah and praised her to Pharaoh; the Aramaic text mentions one of these courtiers by name (Harquenos, or something of the sort), and reproduces his detailed description of the beauty of Sarah's figure. When Sarah is taken away from Abraham, she weeps, and addresses a prayer to God. Thereupon God punishes Pharaoh with a plague which lasts for two years; Lot tells Harquenos the reason of this disaster, and then Pharaoh sends Sarah back again to Abraham.

Such a story clearly owes its origin to pious fantasy, or to a tradition nurtured exclusively on the imagination. It reminds us of stories from apocryphal books such as Enoch, Jubilees and so on, of which we shall shortly have to speak. The story is so full and is so clearly stamped as a literary effort that the fantasy which gave rise to it is probably the author's own, though he may have made use also of elements from oral tradition or folk-lore.

JUBILEES, ENOCH, THE TWELVE TESTAMENTS

Qumran produced fragments of books that had been known for a long time, and which such scholars as Father Lagrange had many years ago attributed to the Essenes. They include works in the apocalyptic style like Jubilees, Enoch, the Testaments of Levi and Nephthali. The discovery of fragments of these works in the caves has at any rate greatly strengthened the suspicion, if they have not made it a certainty, that these books are of Essene origin. The fragments which have been found of the Testaments of Levi and Nephthali show a text which is *not* that of the well-known Testament of the Twelve Patriarchs, but that of the Jewish source which was used by the (Jewish-Christian?) author of the Testaments. 'Apocalyptic' is a strange type of literature: it is anonymous, and presents itself as reproduction of the revelations of some famous person of antiquity, whose words refer chiefly to the time of the real author and to the end of the world, which is to come speedily. A number of apocalyptic writings are known to us because they were transmitted by Christian scribes, mostly in Greek. The style flourished, roughly speaking, between the middle of the second century B.C. and the middle of the second century A.D. The suspicion that there were other apocalypses besides those which survived has been confirmed by the finds in the Qumran caves. So far, however, only fragments have been found, but no texts even to some extent sound. Fragments have already been published from a Book of Noah, the Words of Moses, a Book of Mysteries, a Description of the New Jerusalem, and from other works which have not been more closely identified.

OTHER TEXTS

Among the published texts of Qumran are included some liturgical texts and blessings; the latter are of special interest because they deal in succession with the whole community, the high priest, the priests and the prince of Israel. The 'prince of Israel' is the Messiah from the house of David; being a 'layman', he comes after the high priest and the priests in dignity. They looked forward to a restoration of Israel where the people of God would be ruled by two 'Anointed Ones' in the future: the Messiah from the tribe of Levi and the Messiah from the race of David. The community is arranged on strictly theocratic lines; God rules the people by means of those who know His will best—the priests. The relation of priestly to secular power is probably to be so understood that the priests had charge of the promulgation of God's will, while the civil authorities had to put this will into execution, under close inspection from the priests.

A Prayer of King Nabunaid (Nabonides) published in 1956 reminds us of the cycle of stories told about Daniel. Nabunaid was the last king of Babylon, before the city was taken by Cyrus the Persian in 539 B.C.; after the fall of Babylon, his son Balthassar ruled the city as viceroy. In the course of his prayer, Nabunaid says that while in the oasis of Teima he suffered from an illness which forced him to leave men's company for seven years; he confessed his sins, whereupon a

Jew from the Babylonian exile explained to him what had happened. Now we read in the fourth chapter of Daniel the famous story of the madness of Nabuchodonosor, lasting seven 'periods', which had as its consequence that he was banished from human company. It has been long suspected that this story goes back to what happened in fact to King Nabunaid, who according to the authentic annals of Babylonia lived in Teima for an unknown reason for seven or eight years, during which he left the government of the country to Balthassar. The tradition on which the Prayer of King Nabunaid is based is undoubtedly the same as that which gave rise to the fourth chapter of Daniel, only that at a later stage the well-known name of Nabuchodonosor was substituted for the little-known name of Nabunaid. Besides the 'Prayer of Nabunaid', of which unfortunately only a fragment survives, other small remains of stories in which Daniel figures have been found. All of this is important, because many scholars had long been convinced that the book of Daniel in its present form must have been composed about 165 B.C. and derives from the circle of the Pious, which also gave rise to the Essene movement.

THE COPPER ROLLS

A sensation was caused by the find of two copper rolls, which were discovered in 1952 in Qumran Cave 3. They are the two parts of a single roll, which consisted of three sheets of thin copper each some twelve by thirty inches, riveted end to end along the shorter side. Centuries of oxydization had made the rolls so hard that it was impossible to unwind them to read the text, which was engraved on the inner side. Having considered every possibility and tried all sorts of experiments, the experts finally decided that they could only reach the text by cutting the precious scroll into strips. They proceeded to do so in the early part of 1956 at Manchester, England, and the fact was officially announced on 2 June 1956. The text itself was not published on this occasion, but notice was given that it contains a list of places where hidden treasure was to be found, scattered over most of Palestine. The investigators of the texts at Jerusalem, Father de Vaux and company, consider the list to be a piece of folk-lore to which no real significance is to be attached, but others (Kuhn, Dupont-Sommer) do not agree. They point to stories about the hiding of the temple treasures during the war between the Jews and Romans, A.D. 66–70, and also to the fact that an expensive roll of pure copper hardly seems the proper material on which to inscribe fairy-tales. There must surely have been some very special reason for using such a durable and unusual material to write up a list of hiding-places. Against this, it must be said that lists of secret caches are not generally in-scribed on metal plates which are difficult to conceal. Further, the engraver's hand was not very expert, as I could myself remark when in 1953 I saw the copper rolls in their rolled-up state in the Jerusalem Museum. The writer had dug his point deeply into the soft copper, and a small portion of the text was visible in reverse on the outside. We have here a riddle for which all sorts of solutions may be offered. One might be that the copper plates were originally designed for something else, and that someone engraved the present text on them as the Romans closed in on Jerusalem, in the hope of misleading them when and if they found them. The finders, however, were twentieth-century scholars who do not want to be fooled, and hence are now embroiled in discussion.

A great number of texts have been found besides those given above, but of most of them only the existence is known publicly. Here is a list of the most important: genealogy of priests; *midrash* on the book of Moses; Rule for the distribution of service in the temple among the various classes of priests, over a six-year cycle of 364 days a year; blessings of the Patriarchs, with commentaries; anthology of Messianic texts from Exodus, 2 Samuel, Isaiah, Amos, Psalms, Daniel; Catena (connected series) of Messianic texts; paraphrases of Genesis, Exodus, Samuel; astrological works, e.g. describing the influence of the planets on the formation of the human members; liturgical works; stories connected with the Patriarchs, in the form of free development of the biblical themes; hymns in a style different from that of the Thanksgiving Psalms; a liturgy of the angels; Psalms of Joshua; various prescriptions for ritual purity; a series of pronouncements against those guilty of offences; words of St Michael to the angels; liturgical morning and evening prayers for each day of the week; pseudo-historical texts purporting to come from the Persian period; the heavenly tablets; pseudonymous writing attributed to Jeremiah; texts dealing with Noah and Enoch; blessings; etc.

It is a great pity that only tattered remnants of all this variegated literature survive. But they give us, all the same, some insight into the spiritual life of the sect which is of great importance for our knowledge of the Judaism of the day.

DATING THE MANUSCRIPTS

One last question is that of the date of the manuscripts. How old are they, when were they written? It is far more difficult to decide the age of the texts, that is, when they were composed by their original authors, than the date of the manuscripts, which are usually later than the text—except of course in the case of an autograph, where one is dealing with the actual text as written down by the author himself. The age of biblical texts is a matter for Old Testament studies; the ages of the non-biblical texts can as a rule be decided only by starting from their contents. But to determine the age of manuscripts there are other methods, one old and the other very modern, both of which have been applied to the manuscripts of Qumran.

DATING THE HANDWRITING

The oldest way of finding out the age of a manuscript is by palaeography; that is, the study of the handwriting. In the course of centuries, and even in the course of shorter periods, handwriting is subject to marked changes. A given hand has not only its individual traits, but also, and even more so, the marks of its time and place. Handwriting is a social phenomenon *par excellence*, because it allows us to make contact with other men who are widely separated from us in time and space. Hence the handwriting of one influences that of another, so that gradual changes in writing appear as a social phenomenon, that is, among all at the same time. If then we know how handwriting has developed in a certain setting in the course of time, we have a means of fixing the date of origin for an undated manuscript. With medieval manuscripts from Europe the date can be mostly determined to within fifty years or even more closely. It is only to be expected that after the publication of a number of texts from Qumran scholars should have tried to date them on the basis of the characteristic properties of the handwriting. There was one great difficulty at the beginning, namely, that there was almost no solidly dated material to serve as the basis of comparison. When one has compared hands, and recognized that the writing in one manuscript is similar to that of another, and hence must be of like date, the time of origin of the first manuscript must be known before one can conclude to the date of the second. A second difficulty was that the script of the manuscripts was in block letters, not in real cursive, running hand. Block letters, which are written separately, develop less quickly than a hand where the letters are connected with each other. Further, Eastern handwriting develops much more slowly than ours; even a cursive or semi-cursive hand changes there slowly sometimes; as, for example, the Syrian script. With many Syriac manuscripts it is sometimes impossible to tell when they were written, even to the nearest century, if the scribe has not added the date. A third difficulty in the way of the palaeographical dating of the Qumran manuscripts was the circumstance that apart from the Nash Papyrus, the little material which existed for purposes of comparison consisted of inscriptions on stone or chalk drawings. It is obvious that one does not write on stone in the same manner as on leather or papyrus, since the material used influences the form of the lettering. Also, the date of origin of the Nash Papyrus was being seriously debated.

In spite of all these difficulties, some palaeographers like Birnbaum, Trever, Albright and Cross determined the dates of the Qumran manuscripts on the grounds of the handwriting. Loud protests rang out from many quarters, the scholars objecting that the doubts and difficulties mentioned above were so grave that they thought they must declare impossible a palaeographic dating of the manuscripts. The results achieved, however, seemed to be the same as those arrived at on other grounds (archaeological, etc.), so that one may well say that the palaeographers have won their case. They date the manuscripts of Muraba'at to the second century A.D., the great majority of those of Qumran to the second and first centuries before and the first century after Christ. In the view of the palaeographers, some Qumran texts are from the third century B.C. or even earlier.

A very modern means of dating is the so-called Carbon 14
test, the method of fixing the age of dead organic matter by
measuring the strength of its radio-active carbon content. The
method is a sort of by-product of atomic research, and was
first applied and described by the physicist W. F. Libby at
Chicago. Cosmic rays 'bombard' the atmosphere continually
and split tiny quantities of nitrogen atoms, so that radio-active
Carbon 14 is produced (the normal atomic weight of carbon
being 12). This C 14 is absorbed by plants and animals along
with the ordinary carbon. During life the relation of ordinary
to radio-active carbon in the organism remains constant, but
after death the radio-active falls to normal in a rhythm which
is exactly known: by half in a certain period, by a quarter in
twice that period, by an eighth in four times the period, and so
on. The more time that has passed, the smaller is the propor-
tion of the radio-active carbon which is left. By measuring the
radio-activity of dead matter one can then reckon the date of
the death of the organism, though the longer ago it was, the
greater the margin of inexactitude. The consequence of this
imprecision is that one cannot say when exactly, or about
when, death took place, but that one must indicate two limits
of time within which it occurred. The longer the matter
investigated is dead, the wider must these limits be fixed on
either side.

At present the only way of measuring the radio-activity of
such material is to *burn* enough of it to release a certain mini-
mum quantity (nearly $\frac{3}{4}$ oz.) of its carbon content in a pure
state. Obviously this cannot be done with precious documents
and other objects which have to be preserved. Hence none
of the scrolls was sent to Chicago to have its date determined, but one of the many pieces of linen in which the manuscripts of Cave 1 had been wrapped was submitted to the test.
The two extremes of dating suggested were 167 B.C. and

A.D. 233—a two-hundred-years' margin of error either way. It is now definite that the linen was certainly in the cave in A.D. 68, and it cannot then have been more than twenty-five or fifty years old. Thus the outcome of the Carbon 14 test, A.D. 33 (with a two-hundred-years' margin either way), must be termed absolutely correct in this case!

At the University of Groningen in the Netherlands, a method of measurement has been developed which leaves a margin of inexactitude much smaller than that of Libby's method as it was in January 1951. This offers a way of investigating the Qumran material which has not yet been applied, as far as I know.

Besides the direct method of dating the Qumran manuscripts, there are also indirect ways: the fixing by archaeological methods of the period of the setting in which they were found, and the determination of the period of time which suits best the contents of the texts. This last method can tell us only the earliest period in which the manuscripts can have been copied, the former gives us the latest possible date. Thus we come once more to the years running from about 150 B.C. to A.D. 68, the period in which the community of Qumran flourished.

7

QUMRAN AND CHRISTIANITY

THE relation between the Qumran community and Christianity has formed the subject of a debate which is the most inglorious chapter of the communication of the finds in the desert of Judah to the general public. Long before all the results of the finds and explorations were sufficiently known, or the main lines were fixed, one or two scholars made the disconcerting statement that the finds were to bring about a radical revision in the study of Christian origins. A French scholar, A. Dupont-Sommer, professor at Paris and a great admirer of Renan, found the resemblance between the Teacher of righteousness (as he saw him) and Jesus of Nazareth so extraordinary that he called it 'almost hallucinating' (see his *Aperçus Préliminaires* . . . (1950), p. 122; in the English translation, *The Dead Sea Scrolls*, Oxford (1952), p. 99, 'very impressive'). This view was given wide publicity in popular writings, newspaper interviews and on the radio. Many found it disturbing, and a storm of protest arose, chiefly on the part of believing Christians, in France mostly Catholics. The professor was affected by it and drew in his horns to some extent in succeeding publications, though he never quite retracted.

Later, the American weekly, *The New Yorker*, dispatched one of its ablest journalists to the Dead Sea, to send back from there and from Europe a full account of the finds in the desert. Wilson made up the matter, which was all strange to him, very creditably; he interviewed all the important people, including Dupont-Sommer, and wrote a long and attractive account of it all for *The New Yorker*. This appeared later in expanded form as a book, which was translated into several languages. It was, in his opinion, an incontrovertible fact that the characteristic doctrines of Christianity had gradually and naturally evolved from a dissident sect of Judaism, the community of Qumran. And he came to the conclusion that scholars were deeply disturbed by this discovery. They were, he pointed out, mostly Catholic or Anglican clergymen or Protestant ministers, brought up on the idea that Christianity is a revealed religion or at least a very distinctive and exceptional one, whose origin cannot be explained by the adoption and development of the doctrines of a Jewish sect till then little known, that of Qumran. He thought that pious Jews were also upset at finding that Christianity was historically so closely connected with Judaism as now appeared. He concluded that only persons with no religious affiliations at all, such as a Jewish scholar that he had met in Jerusalem, and, above all, Dupont-Sommer (a former Catholic priest, who has lost the faith), are capable of forming an objective judgment about the significance of the Dead Sea finds.

J. Allegro, a young British scholar belonging to the staff which was studying in Jerusalem the texts found in the desert of Judah and preparing them for publication, announced on the B.B.C. on 23 January 1956 that hitherto unpublished texts from Qumran showed that the Teacher of righteousness was crucified by Alexander Jannaeus, that his body was taken down from the cross and buried, and that his disciples expected the resurrection and second coming of their dead master; Jesus of Nazareth would thus correspond exactly to his Essene model. On 16 March 1956 *The Times* published a letter, signed by five other members of the team engaged at Jerusalem on the study and publication of the scrolls, which declared that they had carefully read once more all the texts and found nothing to support Allegro's assertions. The letter concluded by saying that they were convinced that Allegro 'either has misread the texts or he has built up a chain of conjectures which the materials do not support'.

The text on which Allegro's assertions were based is probably a passage from the Nahum Commentary which was published by him in the course of 1956 in an American periodical. We have discussed it in a previous chapter. It mentions a 'ravening lion' who has hanged men up '[in a manner such as] formerly in Israel [never happened]'. Only the words not in the brackets are actually in the text, the rest were supplied by Allegro to fill up the lacunae. All that can be deduced with probability from the portion that has been preserved is the fact that the 'ravening lion' had men crucified. That is all. It may well be that they were Jews who conspired with Demetrius III against Alexander Jannaeus, if one is allowed to identify the latter with the 'ravening lion'. Not everybody will do so, however; Antiochus Epiphanes has also been suggested who likewise had Jews crucified a century earlier. There is no mention at all in the text of the Teacher of righteousness, but Allegro is an admirer of Dupont-Sommer and has undoubtedly combined his own theory with that of the Paris professor. Allegro's assertions have been weighed in the balance and found not merely too light but without any weight at all.

The radio talk of Allegro was reported in the United States and aroused much discussion there. The Press began to busy itself with the finds from the desert of Judah in a way which it had not done before. A number of publicists claimed that the Dead Sea Scrolls had shaken the foundations of Christianity; articles with such titles, modified by a question-mark, appeared in the Press of many countries, such as the Netherlands. A

Mr A. P. Davies, a Unitarian clergyman, wrote a popular book containing a bitter attack on the American theologians, especially those engaged on the study of the New Testament; he maintained that they had failed in their task of informing the public; they had even deceived it by using expressions which meant one thing to themselves and another to the layman. The texts from the Dead Sea, he said, bound the theologians stringently to revise from top to bottom their views about Christian origins, but they lacked the courage. The publishers' blurb was entirely in keeping with the spirit of Davies's booklet: *The Dead Sea Scrolls: the greatest challenge to Christian dogma since Darwin's theory of evolution!*

The theologians were not at all disturbed, and among the very many scholars who devoted themselves objectively and dispassionately to the study of the texts from the desert of Judah, there is none who has subscribed to the extravagant conclusions put forward by Dupont-Sommer and Allegro and their amateur following. All scholars are convinced that these two gentlemen derive their views partly from untenable translations. To maintain that these two alone are objective because they claim to be free from any religious allegiance, indicates a prejudice which holds as true what one would like to be true. The texts of the desert of Judah are undoubtedly of great importance, especially for those interested in the origins of Christianity, but their importance is on a completely different plane from that which Dupont-Sommer, Allegro and company envisage. In the following pages we give first an outline of the contrasts, and then the resemblances between the sect of Qumran and Christianity.

When, taking them as a whole, we compare the Jewish sect of Qumran with the Christian Church, the great difference between them stands out at once. The community of Qumran is a typical sect which never grew beyond that stage;

Christianity addressed itself, after the famous vision of St Peter at Jaffa (Acts 10) to Jews and Gentiles, while St Paul preached the Gospel chiefly to pagans. In spreading the word of God, the Church used spiritual means: the Spirit of God which inspired her, the impressive power of word and example, the signs which the preachers of the Gospel accomplished. One of the fundamental prescriptions of the new doctrine was the precept of charity, which was to extend to all men. 'You have heard that it hath been said', Jesus proclaimed, 'Thou shalt love thy neighbour and hate thy enemy. But I say to you, Love your enemies . . . and pray for them that persecute and calumniate you: that you may be the children of your Father who is in heaven, who maketh his sun to rise on the good and bad, and raineth upon the just and unjust' (St Matthew 5: 43–5).

The Law of Moses was not abolished by Jesus but fulfilled (St Matthew 5: 17), which involved the abrogation of the many precepts of the so-called ritual law because with the coming of Christianity they had completed their task. Most particularly, Jesus rejected the many prescriptions for ritual purity, especially those laid down by the rabbis: 'Hear ye and understand. Not that which goeth into the mouth defileth a man: but what cometh out of the mouth, this defileth a man. . . . The things which proceed out of the mouth come forth from the heart: and those things defile a man. For from the heart come forth evil thoughts, murders, adulteries, fornications, thefts, false testimonies, blasphemies. These are the things that defile a man. But to eat with unwashed hands doth not defile a man' (St Matthew 15: 10–20).

The Kingdom of God which Jesus came to bring bore no earthly character; weapons are not part of its accoutrements and there can be no question of waging war. Jesus refused to let His disciples defend Him with the sword, and said to Peter: 'Put up again thy sword into its place: for all that take the sword shall perish with the sword' (St Matthew 26: 52). He was the Messiah, the king of the Jews, but His kingship and His kingdom are 'not of this world' (St John 18: 36). Hence He constantly refused to help to work towards the fulfilment of the national aspirations of the Jews; He wished to set up the 'kingdom of David', but in a spiritual manner, not in the fashion for which almost all his Jewish contemporaries hoped and expected, which would involve the termination of the hateful Roman rule. In the new Kingdom of God the Levitical priesthood has no longer any special place; all the prerogatives of Levi, Aaron and their descendants are abolished. Jesus does not even speak of the matter, and the author of the Epistle to the Hebrews demonstrates at length that Jesus is the only priest of the New Law and that the Levitical priesthood has therefore been transferred to him. The same writer goes further and says that just as the priesthood, whose task it was to proclaim the Law of Moses, has been transferred to another, so too another Law is come: 'For the priesthood being translated, it is necessary that a translation also be made of the law' (Hebrews 7: 12). In the new Kingdom of God, ancestry counts no more, but only the gift of the Spirit. St Paul even proclaims that there is no longer any distinction between Jew and Greek, circumcised and uncircumcised.

The above summary embraces some of the most essential characteristics of the Christian Church in the first decades of its existence. When we compare the community of Qumran we get a completely different picture. This is composed of Jews, chiefly descendants of Levi, Judah and Benjamin. Proselytes (converts) may also belong to it, because by their going over to Judaism they became adoptive members of the Jewish people. The universalism of Christianity is completely foreign to the spirit of the sect. Its attitude to the outside world was hostile: the sons of light, as is said in the very beginning of the great Rule, must love their fellows but *hate* all others, the sons of darkness. They must have as little contact with them as possible, and they must one day annihilate them, in a holy war lasting for forty years. This war is no defensive effort which is forced upon them, but a straightforward offensive war, for which they are to prepare themselves by studying strategy and tactics, forging weapons and storing provisions. When the battle is won, God's kingdom on earth is definitely established; its capital is Jerusalem. Two anointed chiefs rule it: the High Priest of the tribe of Aaron, who is first in rank and has supreme control, and the Prince of the race of David, who is responsible for the daily execution of the procedure laid down by the priest.

The Law of Moses is the fundamental law of the community: they must study it uninterruptedly to make sure that they follow it properly and live up to it even in its details. The sabbath is to be kept in all its severity, and it is not even permissible to help a beast which is giving birth on the sabbath or to help the young out of a hole into which it has fallen on the sabbath. Ancestry plays a great part in the community: the priests, the sons of Aaron, have precedence everywhere. This is in fact one of the most striking characteristics of the community; they come back to it again and again. That is not the case with Jesus' apostles; nothing is said of their descent. Matthew, who was also called Levi, was perhaps a levite, if indeed his name proves anything.

A trait of the sect which stands out very markedly was their exaggerated fear of what was ritually unclean. A great number of water cisterns have been discovered in the ruins of Khirbet Qumran, with installations for bathing. We know from Josephus that the Essenes bathed repeatedly to be ritually pure. The Rules of Qumran and Damascus comprise a great number of prescriptions for the members of the group with reference to the preservation of ritual purity. Those who are full members are considered the most completely pure; on many occasions they have to keep themselves apart from those who are already partial members. The greatest 'purity' must be observed at meals, which are never taken unless one has had a complete bath. Here they outdid the Pharisees, who only demanded the washing of the hands, a precept which Jesus and His disciples disregarded (St Matthew 15: 2, 20).

It is clear from the foregoing that the Qumran community and the young Christian Church were two totally different institutions, animated by competely different spirits and radically opposed to each other on the most essential points. There was a deep cleavage between the two, which is certainly the chief reason why the Essenes are never mentioned in the Gospels, although according to Philo and Josephus they belonged to one of the three most important 'sects' of Judaism. When Jesus preached the Gospel, He addressed Himself to 'the lost sheep of the house of Israel' (St Matthew 15: 24); that is, to the Jewish community in Palestine. He came only seldom into contact with Samaritans and non-Jews. The Essenes held aloof from this Jewish community, and on the most essential points their ideals were diametrically opposed to those of Jesus. Also, theirs was a small group. This enables us to explain the fact that they have no particular place in the message of salvation in the Gospel, as it was proclaimed later by the apostles and put in writing by them and their disciples. The Essenes did not busy themselves with the Jews among whom Jesus moved, Jesus did not busy Himself with them, at least not specially enough to have it written down in the Gospel message for the benefit of posterity.

Leaving aside the fundamental difference between the two groups and the fact that early Christianity had no relations with the Essenes important enough to be remembered for posterity, one can still adduce various points of resemblance in subordinate matters. This is not altogether surprising. Christianity did not arise in a vacuum; it did not fall from heaven like a meteor which no one had seen, complete with all its attitudes, customs and practices. Christianity arose in the setting of Judaism, its Founder was born of Jewish ancestors, His apostles and first preachers were Jews. Nor did it shake itself free of Judaism with one swift jerk, because the first Christians still met in the temple, where as late as 57 St Paul had sacrifices offered on behalf of Nazarites, to show that Jewish-Christians were not forbidden to live according to the Old Law (Acts 21: 20–26). When the young Church was sharply divided on the question of whether the heathens who wished to join it were to have themselves circumcised, and were to be forced to keep the whole Law of Moses, the first General Council of the Church came together at Jerusalem in 49 to discuss the matter. After St Peter had proposed that no particular Jewish obligations should be imposed on converted Gentiles, a conciliatory compromise suggested by James was agreed upon; the 'Gentiles' were hereby ordered to abstain from meat that had been offered to idols, from eating blood, and meat with blood in it, and from 'fornication' (by which some exegetes understand marriage within the degrees of kinship forbidden by the Law of Moses). No principle was involved in the decree, which simply aimed at making things easier for the Jews, and it was soon disregarded in practice, as soon as the motive, to spare the Jews, had ceased to exist.

The Church had received the Old Testament as an all-important inheritance from Judaism, and it regarded itself as the legitimate depository of the promises made therein to Israel. The teaching of Jesus and the apostles was indeed new, but it linked up with and continued the old, without which it cannot even be understood. As for ecclesiastical customs and

practices: it is well known that the Church took over many
from the synagogue. This is only natural, for the Church, the
'new Israel', looked on itself as a continuation of the old, and
where there was no reason for changing, it saw no necessity
for it. New forms of organization are generally derived from
older ones which are retained as long as they do not demand
innovation. In matters of organization and social forms, but
also in morals, belief and the presentation of its message, the
Church took with it much of the treasures of Judaism, and that
not only from the Old Testament. The great five-volume
Commentary on the New Testament from the Talmud and Midrash,
by the German scholars H. L. Strack and P. Billerbeck, gives
adequate proof that Judaism, apart from the Bible, offers much
material that can help towards the understanding of the New
Testament and so of Christianity. The discoveries in the
Judaean desert, which have revealed to us a facet of this
Judaism which had been hitherto unknown, have enlarged
this material considerably. And this enhances the importance
of the finds, which in the future will surely interest the
student of the New Testament more than one who confines
himself to the Old.

The most sensational point of resemblance between Qumran
and Christianity, as discovered to the satisfaction of Dupont-
Sommer and his school, is that between the Teacher of
righteousness, great prophet and possible founder of the sect,
and Jesus of Nazareth. Jesus was, to quote Dupont-Sommer,
in many respects an astonishing reincarnation of the Teacher.
Like the latter, He preached repentance, poverty, humility,
love of one's neighbour, chastity. Like him, He prescribed the
Law of Moses, completed by His own revelations, to be
observed in full. Like him, He was God's chosen Messiah and
the Redeemer of the world. Like him, He was the object of the
hostility of the Sadducean priests. Like him, He was con-

demned and put to death, and ascended into heaven to return
at the end of time as the supreme Judge. Like him, He punished
Jerusalem, which had condemned Him to death, by delivering
it to the Romans and causing it to be destroyed. Like him, He
also founded a Church in which the priests are the ministers of
the sacrament of the Sacred Meal; at the head of this Church
there are 'overseers', as among the Essenes, i.e. bishops, and
the ideal of both communities is unity in love. (See Dupont-
Sommer, *The Dead Sea Scrolls* (English translation), p. 99.)
Allegro rounded out this picture with the crucifixion of the
Teacher and his disciples' belief in his resurrection.

Dupont-Sommer said of his series of parallels that they were
'almost hallucinating' (see above, p. 189). No one but himself
and an odd disciple of his has been able to see them in the text
of the scrolls, and practically nothing of them survives a dispassionate consideration of them. A general protest has been
entered against them by students of the texts, but in the meantime they have made their way into radio, television and
popular writing, where they have created an unwholesome
atmosphere, and caused doubts or even disturbance among the
non-experts, who cannot tell who is right and who is wrong.

If one faces facts clearly, and compares the attitude of
Qumran, or the Essenes as the case may be, towards the
Teacher of righteousness, with the relation of the Church
towards Jesus of Nazareth, one touches a point where the deep-
seated differences between the two communities stand out
most unmistakably, as the well-known New Testament
scholar, O. Cullmann, has pointed out. For in the Church,
Jesus, at the right hand of God, is the central figure and the
object of Christian faith. The Church reveres Jesus as Son of
God and His equal, the members of the Church are called
'Christians' after Him. Without Jesus Christ the Church which
He founded is unthinkable and its liturgy robbed of its soul.

What the apostles preached was the Gospel, the good news brought by Jesus Christ; His resurrection was for them the confirmation of the doctrine which they asked others to believe. Jesus was for them the fulfilment of the predictions of the prophets of the old dispensation: the Messiah, which He himself professed to be. With the Teacher of righteousness it is quite otherwise. His name is unknown, his person, as an instrument of God, disappears wholly and entirely behind the divine majesty. No one invokes him, no one worships him after his death, his name and work are not made part of a profession of faith. Contrary to the affirmation of Dupont-Sommer, he did not profess to be the Messiah whom Israel awaited; certainly, in the texts, he is expressly distinguished from the two Messiahs, the priestly Messiah and the Messiah from the house of David, whose coming he awaited as much as his followers. When Dupont-Sommer was writing the account quoted above, the doctrine of the sect about the two Messiahs was not yet quite clear; at present it is incontrovertible, because not merely one but several texts have been found which contain it unmistakably. In the great Rule, for instance, we read that the prescriptions of the community must be observed 'till a prophet comes and the anointed ones [Messiahs] of Aaron and of Israel' (Manual 9: 11). The prophet mentioned here is probably no ordinary one, but a very definite figure whose coming was expected before that of the two Messiahs. The advent of such a prophet was deduced from Deuteronomy 18: 15: 'The Lord thy God will raise up to thee a prophet of thy nation and of thy brethren, like to me [Moses]. Him thou shalt hear.' Belief in his coming is also supposed by the question which the Jews put to John the Baptist after he had denied that he was the Messiah: 'They asked him: What then? Art thou Elias? And he said: I am not. Art thou the prophet? And he answered: No' (St John 1: 21).

If it is correct that the people of Qumran awaited the coming of a very great prophet who was to prepare the way of the two Messiahs and could modify the rules of the community, then this prophet must have been regarded as a greater man than the Teacher. Further, the latter is never called a prophet, he is merely the interpreter of the prophets; God has imparted to him their 'secrets'. It cannot be denied that he looked on his task as a most important one, especially if one accepts him—though this is a supposition which still remains unproved—as the author of the Hymns who speaks therein of his own experiences. There are three places in the Hymns where the author speaks of the commission which he has received:

Thou [God] hast set me as a banner for the elect of righteousness as one who gives instruction in the knowledge of the wonderful mysteries,
to prove those [who cleave to the] truth,
to test those who love exhortation (Thanksgiving Psalms 2: 13 f.).

Through me hast Thou [God] enlightened the face of many, times without number Thou hast displayed Thy might through me,
for Thou hast made known to me Thy holy mysteries.
By thy marvellous decree Thou hast shown Thy power in me, working marvellously in the sight of many for the sake of Thy glory,
and to proclaim Thy might to all that live (Thanksgiving Psalms 4: 27 ff.).

Thou [God] hast made me a father to those that love Thee, the provident guide of all that are a sign (Thanksgiving Psalms 7: 20–21).

In the whole lengthy text of the Psalms that is all that can be quoted with reference to the task of the Teacher, and even then one must ask oneself if it refers to him exclusively, or if it is said of themselves by other enlightened leaders of the sect. A text from the Habacuc Commentary must be added to those quoted above. When explaining the famous words, 'The just shall live by his faith' (Habacuc 2: 4), the commentary says that God will preserve from condemnation, i.e. save, all who have kept the Law faithfully, 'because of their labours and their confidence in the Teacher of righteousness' (Habacuc Commentary 8: 1-2). Instead of 'confidence' one could also read 'faith' in the last part of the text, from which it would then follow that the pious are saved by their faith in the Teacher. When one understands 'faith' in the Pauline sense, one has a parallel with Christianity. But that is not, however, how things stand. To understand the commentary on Habacuc 2: 4 one should not start with St Paul, but with the biblical text of Habacuc. All this means is that the just man shall remain alive and not die a premature death, by reason of his *loyalty* to God (or fidelity, a better translation than 'faith'). Similarly, all who are true to the Teacher, and who have accepted his words and put them into practice, shall also live. That could have been said just as well of Moses and the other prophets, and has nothing to do with faith such as Christians have in Christ. Christ is Himself an object of belief for Christians; in their creeds He takes a place like that of the Father.

The description of the Teacher offered by Dupont-Sommer is taken not from the Qumran scrolls but from the Gospel of Jesus of Nazareth. That the Teacher was put to death is an assumption that still lacks confirmation from the texts; all we read in the Habacuc Commentary is that some great villainy was perpetrated against the Teacher and that he was 're-proved', 'accused', 'denounced'—where a word is used that could also mean 'chastise' (Habacuc Commentary 5: 10). In the Gospel and in the Epistles of St Paul the expiatory death of

Jesus takes the central place, quite different from the still doubtful death of the Teacher in the writings of Qumran.

There is no mention in the Qumran writings of any resurrection of the Teacher or his second coming as Judge. That he 'appeared' after his death to Jerusalem when Pompey took it in 63 B.C., is something that Dupont-Sommer invented on the basis of the following text from the commentary on Habacuc 2:15:

> 'Woe to him that makes his neighbour drink [strong drink], adding thereto his poison [anger], indeed, makes him drunk to regard their feasts': this means the wicked priest, who persecuted the teacher of righteousness to swallow him up in the heat of his anger, in the place of his exile. During the sabbath-rest of the Day of Expiation, he appeared to them to swallow them up and to make them stumble on their day of fast and rest (11:2–8).

Of the appearance of the Wicked Priest in the 'house of exile' (Qumran?) where the Teacher was staying, Dupont-Sommer, and he alone, has made an apparition of the Teacher after his death, on which occasion he is supposed to have 'swallowed up' Jerusalem by delivering it to the Romans on the great Day of Expiation! In offering this audacious and linguistically incorrect explanation, Dupont-Sommer stands quite alone; the text of the commentary is quite innocent of it. Here is a better explanation. At Qumran, they followed a calendar of feasts differing from that of Jerusalem, and therefore celebrated the Day of Expiation on a day that the rest of the Jews did not; on such a day, the Wicked Priest advanced openly on the Teacher and his followers (the text of the commentary used first the singular and then the plural), in order to make them 'stumble' and to 'swallow them up'. Obviously, he wanted to put an end to a celebration which in his eyes was heretical, and to take strong measures against the sect.

Since they believed at Qumran in the resurrection of the

dead, they naturally expected the resurrection of their Teacher. There is, however, no indication that they looked to it as to an extraordinary event because they thought that the Teacher would judge the world. There is only one text, in the Damascus Document, which could possibly be interpreted in this sense. There is mention in that document of those who keep the Law 'till he arises who will teach righteousness in the end of the days' (6: 10–11). The expression 'Teacher of righteousness' (*moreh sedeq* in Hebrew) is avoided here and a phrase somewhat different is used instead (*joreh ha-sedeq* in Hebrew). The exact meaning of the text is not clear; there is something to be said for the explanation that it alludes to the appearance of the great prophet for whom they waited. They certainly were not thinking of the Teacher of righteousness if the use of a different title was *deliberate*.

Once Dupont-Sommer had promoted his Teacher of righteousness to the status of Messiah, he also proclaimed him 'Saviour of the World'. This was done on the basis of a text from the Testament of Levi (see *The Jewish Sect of Qumran and the Essenes*, English translation of *Nouveaux Aperçus* (1954), p. 47), which is translated from the Greek as follows:

And behold, I [Levi] have no part in your guilt and the crime that you will commit in the end of the ages *against the Saviour of the world*, misleading Israel and bringing upon it great calamities from God. You will behave in Israel in a sinful manner, so that [God] will bear with Jerusalem no more on account of your iniquity, but shall rend the veil of the temple that your shame may not remain hidden. And you shall be scattered in captivity among all the peoples, and there you shall be an object of shame and curse (Testament of Levi, Greek text, chapter 10).

Another text from the same book reads as follows:

I [Levi] know, my children, that at the end of the ages you will commit sin against the Lord, you will lay hands *on him* wickedly, and you will be an object of scorn among all the peoples. Your father Israel is guiltless of the sin of the high priests *who have laid hands upon the Redeemer of the world* . . . (Testament of Levi, Greek text, chapter 14).

The book of The Testament of the Twelve Patriarchs, from which the above quotations are taken, is extant in several different editions. The words printed in italics in the two passages cited above are held by most scholars to be Christian interpolations. The Netherland scholar M. de Jonge, however, in a full-length study of the text published at Leyden in 1953, has argued very ably that it is incorrect to speak of interpolations. His argument is that the whole book of the Testaments is a Christian work written about A.D. 200, but making copious use of Jewish material. According to Milik, one of the most distinguished editors of the texts from the desert of Judah, this view has been confirmed by the discoveries of Qumran. Among the tens of thousands of fragments that have been found, texts of Jubilees or Enoch are recognizable enough, but absolutely nothing has been found which corresponds to the text of the Twelve Testaments, *as we know it in the Greek* translation(s).

When one considers the great quantity and diversity of the literature of which remains have been found, says Milik, one cannot but conclude that the book of the Twelve Testaments, in the form hitherto known, did not form part of the writings of Qumran. And in fact the remains of a very lengthy text of a Testament of Levi and a Testament of Nephthali have been found, but they are not on all fours with the Greek texts. Milik regards this as a confirmation of the thesis of de Jonge, to which he fully subscribes, and thinks that a Christian author made use of a very full Hebrew text of the Twelve Testaments in order to compose the well-known apocryphal book which goes by the same name. If this is correct, it may be assumed that we now have found some of the material whose existence was postulated by de Jonge in his thesis. We may add that even if de Jonge is wrong, it is, to say the least of it, extremely doubtful and improbable that the sayings about the 'Redeemer of the World' are pre-Christian, Jewish or Essene. It is therefore most regrettable that Dupont-Sommer should have used such texts, in a work destined for the general public, to prop up his hypothesis.

With that, there is not much left of the parallelism between the Teacher and Jesus of Nazareth, since the most important elements appear conspicuous by their absence. And we have not as yet considered less important points, such as the supposed agreement in the preaching of charity. We have already seen what this meant at Qumran: love for the members of the group, hatred towards all others. The ideal of chastity which Jesus proclaimed was also radically different from that of the Qumran brotherhood as explained above. Jesus praised celibacy, as did the Essenes, but from quite different motives, as we shall show later. One more observation in conclusion. To build up as great a similarity as possible between Jesus and the Teacher of righteousness, one of the elements invoked is the three texts cited above from the Thanksgiving Hymns. The texts in question, which are said to be written by the Teacher, show that their author was a successful exponent of revealed truths. But in the same Hymns there occur about ten other passages where the author speaks about his sins, claiming that God has granted him forgiveness for them. We quote one of these passages, from the very same psalm which is supposed to offer a 'parallel' to Jesus:

> For I think of my sins and the iniquity of my fathers,
> as evil-doers transgress Thy covenant,
> miserable offenders against Thy word.
> I said: because of my sins have I been abandoned and the covenant
>   with Thee is bereft of force (Thanksgiving Psalms 4: 34–35).

Jesus was conscious of His sinlessness; His sufferings were not to satisfy for His own sins, but to expiate the sins of others. In full consciousness of this, He challenged the Jews, according to the well-known text of St John 8: 46, 'Which of you shall convince me of sin?' Jesus knew Himself to be the Messiah and Son of God, the sinless one who takes death freely upon Himself as the propitiatory sacrifice for sins, who preached in His Gospel love for all men, even towards enemies, and who went directly contrary to the views on ritual purity held by His contemporaries. What an immense difference there is between Him and the Teacher of righteousness, who knows that he is a sinful man and who is conscious that he can only do a good act when and in so far as God helps him, who commands his followers to hate the sons of darkness and prescribes numerous ritual washings for his disciples, who desires them to hold themselves aloof from everything and everybody that is unclean, who is not the Messiah and who does not seek death, and who has to his credit not one of the marvellous deeds of which the four Gospels are full. That Jesus of Nazareth was an astonishing 'reincarnation' of the Teacher is completely out of the question. If, however, one were to suppose that this were after all true, there would still be no reason for any Christian's being disturbed. Because Christians believe that Jesus is risen from the dead and is the Son of God: and they recognize this as the predominant and decisive difference between Him and the still anonymous Teacher. The Teacher did not rise from the dead, nor is he Son of God like Jesus. Besides these capital differences there are points where a comparison may possibly be instituted, but they are of completely subordinate interest. The liberal Protestant looks on Jesus as an outstanding religious person-ality, but a man like ourselves for all that. His doctrine would then be completely human in origin, and it would not be altogether surprising to find it linked up with earlier models. Some perhaps may feel wounded in their dignity when it appears, or seems to appear, that Christianity is not so original as they thought: but the authority of Christian doctrine is not greater or less because it claims originality in a greater or a lesser degree. It would hardly be in keeping with the Gospel for the Christian to pride himself on 'not being like the rest of men'.

We give now a number of points on which there is a resemblance between Qumran and the New Testament, or between the sect and the Christian Church, as the case may be. We select only the most notable points out of the many which space forbids us to touch upon.

Strict community of goods was the law in the Qumran brotherhood; personal property was excluded. This sharing of property did not extend to all Essene groups; it seems to have been left to the choice of the individual whether he joined a group which followed a strict rule, or a group which had a milder one, more in accordance with everyday life. The same was true of the Church in the time of the apostles. The most ancient group of believers 'had but one heart and one soul. Neither did any one say that aught of the things which he possessed was his own: but all things were common unto them' (Acts 4: 32). But this was no universal obligation, as may be seen from the story of Ananias and Saphira, who sold some land but paid in only part of the price to the apostles, though pretending that they were surrendering everything. They were punished for their deceit, after Peter had expressly declared that they had been free to contribute the money or not. But in their conduct they had 'lied not to men, but to God' (Acts 5: 4).

It is clear that Jesus, and the apostle St Paul likewise, recommended celibacy as an excellent way of life. The apostle also gives the reasons: 'He that is without a wife is solicitous for the things that belong to the Lord: how he shall please God. But he that is with a wife is solicitous for the things of the world: how he may please his wife' (1 Corinthians 7: 32–3). According to Philo and Josephus, the reason the Essenes did not marry was that marriage was the cause of quarrels and disunion, and because women would corrupt men by their misconduct. One asks oneself were these the real reasons or merely face-saving ones, possibly chosen with a view to flattering certain male readers among the Greeks. The true reason is almost certainly none other than fear of contracting ritual impurity.

According to the Law of Moses, sexual intercourse renders people unclean. The woman who gives birth to a child remains unclean for forty days if it is a boy, and eighty days if it is a girl. The Essenes were not the only Jews who tried on this account to avoid sexual intercourse as much as possible. Several rabbis are praised for having used marriage exclusively in the service of the precept of Genesis 1: 28, 'Increase and multiply'. Josephus says of the Essenes that the married ones abstained from intercourse during the period of pregnancy, in order to show that they did not look on pleasure but on the begetting of children as the end of matrimony. Hence any resemblance between Essene and Christian ideals with regard to celibacy seems to be superficial; the aims are quite different in each case. Furthermore, Christianity rejects the idea that the sexual intercourse which God has instituted could make men 'unclean' even within the bonds of matrimony, though admittedly this ancient attitude influenced for a long time the estimation of sexual life among Christians. Even today this influence has not entirely spent its force.

A college of twelve laymen and three priests was at the head of the Qumran community. As we have already said, it is not clear whether the three priests were part of the total of twelve or were outside it. In the former case, the resemblance with the college of twelve apostles, where three had special prerogatives, would be striking. And John the Baptist, with whom Jesus maintained close relations, was of priestly family. The Christian community of Jerusalem was directed by 'the apostles and presbyters' (Acts 15: 4, 6, 22, 23) who also had charge of the whole Church. This reminds us of the college of twelve or fifteen, as the case may be, which along with the priests and elders were the most prominent people in the Qumran community.

Some Christian communities were ruled by a college of 'presbyters' at the head of which was the *episcopos*. The Greek word means 'overseer', 'he who is in charge', and became 'bishop' in English, just as the Greek word for 'ancient', 'elder', which is *presbyteros*, became 'priest'. In the Acts of the Apostles, the difference between 'bishop' and 'presbyter' is not always equally clear, but we can nevertheless form a picture of the organization of the community. Now it is remarkable that there was a *mebaqqer* at the head of the Qumran community; the word likewise signifies 'overseer', 'inspector' (see above, page 135). To become a Christian, one had to undergo a period of probation, the so-called catechumenate, though this was not in force at the very beginning, but came in only somewhat later. The community of Qumran also imposed a period of probation, sometimes a double or even three-fold period, on its would-be members. Since the probationary period was organized on a totally different basis at Qumran, the probation shows up the differences rather than the resemblances between the two communities: a period of probation is in itself nothing remarkable and occurs everywhere.

The sect looked on itself as the 'true Israel', as did the Church. St Paul calls the Jews 'Israel according to the flesh' (1 Corinthians 10: 18), while he calls the Church 'the Israel of

God' (Galatians 6: 16). St Peter, using expressions from the Old Testament, speaks in his First Epistle of Christians as 'a chosen generation, a kingly priesthood, a holy nation, a purchased people' (1 Peter 2: 9). This is in striking agreement with what the Qumran community thought of itself, especially with regard to the use of the expression 'priesthood'. Its ideals were indeed priestly; priests gave the lead in everything and the members tried to be as like them as possible, by taking upon themselves the rules of ritual purity which bound the priests. None the less, the difference here between the Church and the brotherhood remains great. The difference between Jew and non-Jew was eliminated in the Church, but not at Qumran. The proselyte, or heathen convert, who joins the Jewish people, becomes a member of that people and leaves his own; but in Israel he ranks below those who are children of Abraham and Isaac by birth and not by adoption. And as regards the priestly ideals: this is not a trend exclusive to Essenism and Christianity. It is already found in the Old Testament, where the prophet speaks as follows to an Israel that has been restored and brought back to its own land: 'You shall be called priests of Yahweh, ministers of our God shall you be named' (Isaiah 61: 6). Among the chosen people, the priests were especially chosen by God. Hence the imagery of the priesthood was used to stress the notion of election.

Ritual washings, which aimed at self-purification, were practised at Qumran. According to the doctrine of the great Rule, purification does not follow automatically upon ablution, because, as it says, 'no one can be purified if he has not sorrow for his sins' (Manual 5: 13–14). John the Baptist administered his baptism to those who had shown sorrow for their sins; it was a sign that they were determined to live good lives in the future. It is by baptism that one becomes a member

of the Christian Church; it can be administered only once
and is regarded as the symbol of passing from an 'old' life to a
'new'. The difference between the Christian practice and
that of Qumran is much greater than the similarity because at
Qumran purifications were going on continually, to wash
away minor impurities; Christian baptism is administered
only once because it makes a man a new creation.

A number of scholars have paid great attention to the meals
of Qumran, in which parallels to the Holy Eucharist of
Christianity have been seen. A text of Josephus has led many
scholars to assume that the Essenes held a sacred meal twice a
day, at which bread and one other dish were eaten. The Two-
Column Document of Qumran mentions a meal where bread
and wine are set out and where the two anointed ones (the high
priest and the son of David) take part, giving the impression
that it is a very special meal in the coming Messianic kingdom.

Any possible resemblance to the Eucharist or at least to the
love-feast (the so-called *agape*) of ancient Christianity does
not take us very far. Leaving aside the question of the original
relation of love-feast and Eucharist in the early Church, we
can see clearly from the very oldest sources, the Gospels and
the First Epistle of St Paul to the Corinthians (11: 17–34), that
the Christian Eucharist was a sacred meal which was celebrated in memory of the death of the Lord: 'As often as you
shall eat this bread and drink the chalice, you shall show the
death of the Lord, until he come' (1 Corinthians 11: 26).
There is not the least hint that the daily meals of the Essenes
had a similar memorial character: on the contrary, it is
practically certain that they had not, because meals with a
special significance are usually confined to special occasions.
Furthermore, Christians have always regarded the bread and
wine taken at the Lord's Supper as the body and blood of the
Lord, either in the mysterious Real Presence of the glorified

Christ (as in the Catholic Church) or in figure and force. The Gospels leave no doubt of this: 'And whilst they were eating, Jesus took bread; and blessing broke and gave to them, and said: Take ye. This is my body. And having taken the chalice, giving thanks, he gave it to them. And they all drank of it. And he said to them: This is my blood of the new testament, which shall be shed for many' (St Mark 14: 22–24). Such views, which are the centre and essence of the Christian celebration of the Eucharist, are completely missing among both the Essenes and the community of Qumran.

In addition, there is grave doubt that the daily meals of the Essenes were really sacred meals at all. The scholars who have assumed that they were, seem in all probability to have been misled by certain expressions of Josephus who describes the daily meals of the Essenes and *compares* them with the sacred meals of paganism. Further, Josephus does not speak of bread and wine, but of bread and some other food prepared by the cook. He does not mention wine. Bread was always eaten at Jewish meals in the time of Christ, so much so that the expression 'to eat bread' has in Hebrew the same meaning as 'have a meal'. Whenever it was to be had, they used wine mixed with water as their drink, and it could certainly never be omitted on festive occasions. Bread and wine were quite ordinary at table, and there was nothing special about them. The fact that they are mentioned in connexion with the meal to which the high priest and the 'Messiah of Israel' sit down, carries of itself no special weight. Furthermore, the text of the Two-Column Document as a whole does not give the impression that it means to describe a sacred or 'Messianic' banquet. The document is concerned with the order of precedence in the community, and the right or prerogative of pronouncing the first blessing and thanksgiving at table. The high priest has the honour, and only then the 'Messiah of Israel', if he happens to be present. The text also lays down expressly that this rule applies to every meal at which at least ten persons are present: the priest is always first in rank, it is he who blesses the food and thanks God for it.

It may be that the Essenes held sacred meals, on the analogy of the sacred sacrificial meals of the Jews in general; but up to the present no resemblance to the Christian Eucharist is apparent, and it seems most unlikely that any such resemblance will ever come to light.

ST JOHN

We meet in the Gospel according to St John certain expressions and concepts which are directly paralleled in the Qumran writings. No one can miss the distinction which St John makes in his Gospel between what he calls 'light' and 'darkness', 'truth' and 'lie', 'life' and 'death'. He treats light, truth and life as kindred and often identical concepts, and the same holds good for darkness, falsehood and death. The meaning of these expressions is very close to that of similar ones in the Qumran texts, and they occur there a number of times in practically the same sense. For St John, the coming of Jesus is like a light from heaven, which shines in the darkness of the world: 'In him was life, and the life was the light of men; and the light shineth in darkness: and the darkness did not embrace it' (St John 1: 4-5). This is the theme with which the Gospel begins. It sees God and His world as two kingdoms or domains, one of light and one of darkness. Human society, the 'world', belongs in fact to the kingdom of darkness into which only a little light streams. This dualistic mode of expression recurs throughout the whole Gospel. The expression 'light' occurs twenty-five times, the word 'darkness' ten times, and nearly always in a metaphorical sense. We even meet the phrase 'sons of light' once: 'Whilst you have the light believe in the light, that you may be the children [sons] of light' (St John 12: 36). We find the same expression in St Luke: 'The children [sons] of this world are wiser in their generation than the children [sons] of light' (16: 8), as also in St Paul: 'For you were heretofore darkness, but now light in the Lord. Walk then as children of the light. For the fruit of the light is in all goodness and justice and truth' (Ephesians 5: 8–9).

In the Gospel of St John, Jesus is the light from which all light radiates that is in this world; in opposition to this is 'the world', of which the devil is 'father': 'You [the Jews addressed by Jesus] are of your father the devil: and the desires of your father you will do. He was a murderer from the beginning: and he stood not in the truth, because truth is not in him. When he speaketh a lie, he speaketh of his own: for he is a liar and the father thereof' (St John 8: 44). With these words Jesus brands those of His hearers who refuse to believe in Him as 'sons of the devil'; if He had called them 'sons of darkness' in the sense common to the writings of Qumran, He would have said nothing different, since His whole mode of expression comes to the same thing. In the Qumran system, the 'sons of darkness' are in fact completely at the mercy of the evil spirits at whose head is the Belial who is also known from the New Testament. Like Qumran, too, the Gospel of St John makes no distinction between Jews and heathens who refuse to believe in Jesus; all are comprehended in the expression 'the world' or 'this world'.

In the First Epistle of St John, the 'sons of God' are expressly contrasted with 'the sons of the devil' (1 John 3: 10). Another passage of the same Epistle discusses the 'discernment of spirits':

> Dearly beloved, believe not every spirit, but try the spirits if they be of God: because many false spirits are gone out into the world. By this is the spirit of God known. Every spirit which

confesseth that Jesus Christ is come in the flesh is of God: And every spirit that dissolveth Jesus is not of God. And this is Antichrist, of whom you have heard that he cometh: and he is now already in the world. You are of God, little children, and have overcome him. Because greater is he that is in you, than he that is in the world. They are of the world. Therefore of the world they speak: and the world heareth them. We are of God. He that knoweth God heareth us. He that is not of God heareth us not. By this we know the spirit of truth and the spirit of error (1 John 4: 1–6).

It is hardly necessary to prove that this passage, in so far as the expressions are concerned (apart from the position which *Jesus* occupies in them), may be placed side by side with the famous section of the great Rule of Qumran which deals with the two spirits. The spiritual climate is the same.

Parallels to the doctrine of the two spirits and the two ways as taught at Qumran did not stop with the New Testament. The Didache (Teaching of the Twelve Apostles), an ancient Christian document from about A.D. 150 or earlier, begins with six chapters in which the Christian ethic is propounded by means of the metaphor of two ways, or angels, of life and death, light and darkness. These chapters were in existence before the Didache was written, and were incorporated into it by the editor or compiler from a source already in circulation. The ancient Christian document called (incorrectly) the Epistle of Barnabas, which is not later than A.D. 140, also contains chapters where similar views are put forward. Are we to discern here the traces of the Qumran school? Or must we assume the existence of a spiritual climate, a set of thoughts and attitudes, or perhaps even written sources from which all alike have drawn? This must remain an open question as long as literary dependence cannot be proved; that is, as long as it cannot be demonstrated that the author of one document made use of the work of another and borrowed expressions and characteristic ideas from another's *writing*. And such proof is still not forthcoming.

ST PAUL

In the Epistles of St Paul we also come upon expressions and lines of thought which correspond to the writings of Qumran. There is, of course, first and foremost a deep-seated difference. The unique and ubiquitous predominance which Christ takes in the thought and in the life of St Paul has no real parallel at all at Qumran. But if we prescind from this, we do find some important Pauline ideas in the writings of Qumran. We have already remarked above that St Paul is also acquainted with the expression 'sons of light' and the lines of thought which go with it. One text is very clear in this regard: 'What fellowship hath light with darkness? And what concord hath Christ with Belial?' (2 Corinthians 6: 14–15). More important is the Pauline thesis that man can perform no good action of himself, and that he is entirely dependent on God for all the good he does, which is one of the central thoughts of the Qumran Hymns.

> Because the way of man is not his own,
> man does not dispose his own steps;
> because judgment belongs to God,
> it is He who makes perfect man's conduct.
> By His knowledge comes all that happens,
> all that is comes about by His purpose
> and nothing comes to be without Him (Manual 11: 10–11).

One can compare this and similar sayings with St Paul's: 'Not that we are sufficient to think any thing of ourselves, as of ourselves: but our sufficiency is from God' (2 Corinthians 3: 5). One of the principles of the Qumran community is that a man

is free to choose to follow the promptings of the good or of
the evil spirit; the choice is not irrevocable and so he retains
his freedom, but as soon as he has made his decision, and as
long as it has not been revoked, he does all that he is bidden
by the spirit to whom he has surrendered himself. If a man
behaves well, he does so through the power of the good spirit,
which is as much as to say through the power of God; of
himself he can do nothing good, and he is even sinful. This
reminds us of such sayings as: 'Truly, to will is present with
me, but to accomplish that which is good, I find not. For the
good which I will, I do not . . .' (Romans 7: 18–19). 'With
fear and trembling work out your salvation. For it is God
who worketh in you, both to will and to accomplish, according to his good will' (Philippians 2: 12–13). 'By the grace of
God I am what I am. And his grace in me hath not been void:
but I have laboured more abundantly than they: yet not I, but
the grace of God with me' (1 Corinthians 15: 10). The word
'will' is used in a different sense in each of the two first of these
quotations; in the first it stands for 'I should like to will [but
do not]'; in the second it is a very general will to action, which
according to the apostle is brought about in man by God
when He desires to accomplish his salvation. One has the
impression that St Paul goes even further than the men of
Qumran were ready to do; even the good act of man's will, he
seems to say, is a gift of God. 'To will' in this case means
primarily, no doubt, to have the good desires which God
arouses in man, because for the apostle 'to will' remains a
somewhat vaguely defined concept, as appears from the first
quotation. The resemblance to Qumran is undeniable.
However, both go back to the Old Testament which is almost
one long plea for the recognition of Yahweh's causal influence
on all that happens, and where we can read the famous con-
fession: 'Yahweh . . . all our works hast thou wrought for us'

(Isaiah 26: 12). In later times, however, the Jews were inclined to lay an ever greater stress on man's free will and so on the value of 'works'; that is, the actions which a man himself accomplishes. At Qumran another tendency comes to the fore, and it is even more strongly marked in St Paul. The question of the relations between the doctrine of St Paul and that of Qumran must again remain open. But one feels that there is a relation, though it is impossible to say whether it is direct or indirect.

In the doctrine of predestination or predetermination there is also agreement between St Paul and Qumran. In one of the hymns, the author first acknowledges that it is God who enables men to perform good works, and then goes on to say that God had determined these actions before He created men, and that no one can alter God's decrees. Then he addresses himself to God and says:

> God has created the just man [here a word is missing] and from the womb Thou hast prepared him for the time of Thy good pleasure to uphold Thy covenant . . . and to [a word missing] him with Thy great mercy, and in all his straits to open his soul unto eternal salvation and peace where naught is lacking, where Thou exaltest his glory above the flesh. But the wicked Thou hast made for . . . [the day of Thy good pleasure?—the text is incomplete]; from the womb Thou hast predestined them for the day of slaughter, for their doings are not good . . . and nothing that Thou hast commanded is pleasing to them and their heart is set on what Thou hatest. . . . Thou hast established them to execute dire judgments upon them in the sight of all Thy creation, to be a sign . . . eternally, that . . . [all?] may know Thy glory and the greatness of Thy power (Thanksgiving Psalms 15: 15–21).

When one reads along with the text cited above the famous passage from the ninth chapter of St Paul's Epistle to the

Romans, the resemblance is very striking. God chooses those whom He wills, it says; He prepares them and destines them for glory; He tolerates the wicked and manifests His power by punishing them. One can see that the doctrine of predestination is the same in both cases. St Paul goes perhaps even further, at least in his way of expressing himself. Because though at Qumran they said that God knows the evil deeds of men beforehand, tolerates them for a while and finally punishes them, they avoided saying that God exercised any sort of positive influence on such evil; whereas St Paul uses expressions of which one might say at first sight that they go further. In the ninth chapter of the Epistle to the Romans, referred to above, he puts himself the difficulty, that if the good acts of men depend on God, He cannot reproach sinners with their evil ways. The answer is that man cannot make any reproaches to God: 'Shall the thing formed say to him that formed it: Why hast thou made me thus? Or hath not the potter power over the clay of the same lump, to make one vessel unto honour and another unto dishonour? What if God, willing to show his wrath and to make his power known, endureth with much patience vessels of wrath, fitted for destruction, that he might show the riches of his glory on the vessels of mercy which he hath prepared unto glory. . . ?' (Romans 9: 20–23). To support his argument, the apostle appeals to a number of texts from the Old Testament. The views current at Qumran are to be attached to the same Old Testament.

There is also agreement between St Paul and some texts from Qumran with regard to the apostle's views about the 'mysteries' of God. As we have explained in a previous chapter, when they spoke of mysteries at Qumran they meant for the most part the divine decrees and plans, part of which were contained, in mysterious fashion, in the words of the prophets; the Teacher of righteousness knows these secrets by means of divine revelation. At the end of the Epistle to the Romans, the apostle speaks of how Jesus Christ is proclaimed to the world; it is done 'according to the revelation of the mystery which was kept secret from eternity, which is now made manifest by the scriptures of the prophets, according to the precept of the eternal God, known among all nations for the obedience of faith . . .' (Romans 16: 25–27).

The Heidelberg professor, Dr Kuhn, has pointed out in several publications and lectures that the texts in the Epistles of St Paul, which deal with morals and demand the exercise of various virtues, can be supplied with a number of parallels from the Qumran texts. So far, however, the agreement is nowhere so close that one must assume a direct dependence; one should rather speak of a certain resemblance in the spiritual atmosphere.

Comparisons have also been made between the way the Old Testament is interpreted in the New, and that which is found in the writings of Qumran; some scholars have claimed to find the same method in both. In each case, it is said, there is question of an inspired or revealed exegesis. God had given the Teacher of righteousness insight into the secrets of the prophets; Jesus 'enlightened the understanding' of the disciples 'that they might understand the scriptures' (St Luke 24: 45). That there is a resemblance is undeniable. But for anyone who believes that Jesus is the Messiah, and that the prophecies of the Old Testament have been fulfilled in Him, there is also a great difference, which primarily concerns the facts of the matter. But even from the point of view of method, complete agreement is equally lacking. The commentator on Habacuc reads in a perfectly arbitrary fashion the events of his own day into the text of the ancient prophet, in a manner that flouts the rules of even the most artificial exegesis. However, one can hardly reproach him with this, because the commentator did not aim at giving any authentic exegesis, as far as one can see, but only at revealing secrets which were perhaps in his view not known even to the prophet. With this, all harmony between prophetic text and 'fulfilment' breaks down.

The manner in which the Old Testament is presented as fulfilled in the New is not everywhere the same. It is mostly not a matter of minor details, as at Qumran, whose commentaries remind us of the pseudo-revelations of Jewish apocalyptic, but of the great lines. In their exegesis, the writers of the New Testament always keep before their eyes the harmony between Old and New Testaments; sayings from the Old Testament, when applied to situations from the New Testament, take on a new meaning for them, which must, however, harmonize with the old. To take an example: in the Old Testament the people of Israel is represented as the servant of God, and once even as the son of God, while in the New Testament this is primarily Jesus. Hence various sayings which in the Old Testament refer to the people, are applied to Jesus in the New. Osee (Hosea) 11: 1, cited in St Matthew 2: 15, offers a well-known example. Just as God's son Israel was called out of Egypt by God, so is God's Son, Jesus of Nazareth. The possibility of this application is based on the thought that the people of Israel had come to perfection in Jesus; he is the best, the most exalted son of the chosen people, and anything good that can be said of the people, he can call his own in a much higher sense. Hence it can be said that in him is fulfilled the prophetic word: 'Out of Egypt have I called my son' (Osee 11: 1). He who reads the text must apply it to Jesus, so that it gains a higher sense, which links up harmoniously with the old. Because all that was still imperfect in Israel was brought to perfection in Jesus. Texts from the Old Testament are quoted in the New to prove that Jesus is really the Messiah promised by the prophets, and also to show the harmony that joins the two orders of salvation. The Jew who became a Christian must know that there was no loss but only gain.

These few remarks do not exhaust all that might be said about the way or ways that the Old Testament is quoted in the New. The subject would need a book, rather than a few lines in a work where it can only be touched upon. Suffice it to say that in spite of resemblances there is nevertheless a profound difference, in method and in content, between the principles of the New Testament and the exegesis of Qumran.

As has been said, we have confined ourselves in the preceding discussion to the most important points of difference and agreement between Qumran and Christianity. Agreements are marked enough to deserve serious study and they are of great interest to the student of the New Testament. The New Testament scholar, O. Cullmann, has said that the writings of Qumran teach us that various elements in Christianity, once attributed to the influence of Greek culture and Hellenism, can now be explained as the outcome of trends within Judaism itself. This is said to be of particular importance for the explanation of the Gospel of St John and the Epistles of St Paul. Whatever one thinks of this, it has certainly become clearer than before that Christianity did not arise in a vacuum but that it took over its form of organization and part of its moral teaching from organizations and ethics already in existence. The task of recording agreements also brings to light the great and profound difference. Anyone who wishes to convince himself fully should read the texts from Qumran, and after that the Gospels and the rest of the New Testament. His verdict will not be doubtful. Qumran and the New Testament speak each their own language.

READING MATTER

The literature on the texts of Qumran is extensive, both in scientific and in popular publications. In three surveys published in the *Proceedings of the Near Eastern and Egyptian Society, Ex Oriente Lux*, Nos. 11 (1949–50), 12 (1951–2), 14 (1955–6), the author has discussed the scientific literature on Qumran and given the complete titles of about 600 publications, with a number of photographic plates. See:

'The ancient manuscripts of the desert of Judah in the light of contemporary written documents' (in Dutch), *Proceedings*, 11, pp. 41–71, Plates 7–18.

'The ancient manuscripts found by the Dead Sea in 1947' (in Dutch), *Proceedings*, 12, pp. 221–48.

'The manuscripts found since 1947 in the desert of Judah' (in French), *Proceedings*, 14, pp. 84–116.

The reader is referred to these articles for fuller information and detailed bibliography.

The following works are recommended as a general introduction to the subject:

H. BARDTKE, *Die Handschriftenfunde am Toten Meer*, Berlin, 1953 [176 pp.].

M. BURROWS, *The Dead Sea Scrolls*, London, 1956 [xiii+ 435 pp.].

G. MOLIN, *Die Söhne des Lichtes*, Vienna-Munich, 1954 [254 pp.].

C. T. FRITSCH, *The Qumran Community, its History and Scrolls*, New York, 1956 [147 pp.].

G. GRAYSTONE, *The Dead Sea Scrolls and the Originality of Christ*, London, 1956 [117 pp.].

G. VERMÈS, *Discovery in the Judaean Desert, The Dead Sea Scrolls and their Meaning*, New York, 1956 [238 pp.].

J. T. MILIK, *Dix ans de découvertes dans le Désert de Juda*, Paris, 1957 [121 pp.].

H. H. ROWLEY, *The Zadokite Fragments and the Dead Sea Scrolls*, Oxford, 1952 [xii+133 pp.].

C. BURCHARD, *Bibliographie zu den Handschriften vom Toten Meer*, Berlin, 1957 [xv+118 pp.].

The above works give a general view of the question, and most of them (Bardtke, Burrows, Molin, Vermès) offer complete or partial translations of the most important texts.

The first complete translation to appear is:

T. H. GASTER, *The Scriptures of the Dead Sea Sect*, London, 1957 [359 pp.]. This translation is somewhat free in places, and very much in the author's own idiom, but is to be recommended.

INDEX

INDEX

Aelia Capitolina (Jerusalem), 45
Agrippa, 45, 81
Ahriman, 95
Ahura Mazda, 95, 96, 100
Ain Feshkha, 3, 62, 69, 84, 150
Albright, Prof. William F., 18, 186
Allegro, J., 8, 190, 191, 192, 199
American School of Oriental
  Research, 18
Andromache of Euripides, 27
Antigonus, 44, 59
Antiochus IV, Epiphanes, 34, 36,
  59, 61, 169
Antiochus VII, Sidetes, 38, 66
Antiochus VIII, 60
Antipater, 40
Apocalyptic writings, 180–1
Apsu, 95
Aristeas, 161; *Epistle of,* 35
Aristobulus I, 38, 59
Aristobulus II, 40, 41, 42, 59
Ashton, Brigadier, 20
Assur, 104
Athanasius, Mar. *See* Samuel
Atyehs, 161
Augustine, St, 92, 138
Avesta, the, 96

Bardai, Jacob, 5
Bar Kochba (Bar Koseba), 28;
  revolt of, 45; acclaimed as
  Messiah, 85–7
Bedouin, 3
Beirut, American Methodist Uni-
  versity at, 14
ben Mathathias, Joseph, 46. *See
  also* Josephus, Flavius
Benoît, Fr, 17

ben Sirach, Jesus, 57, 93. *See also*
  Ecclesiasticus
Bible Commentaries, discovery of,
  165–70
Biblical Archaeologist, The, 9, 14
Biblical texts, discovery of, 151–65
Bnê miqra. See Karaites
Boulos, 7–8
Brownlee, Dr W., 19
Burrows, Prof. Millar, 18, 170

Canon Law, Code of, 142
Catholic Biblical Association, 164
Chenoboskion, library of, 23
Coins, 66, 67–8
*Commentary on the New Testament
  from the Talmud and Midrash*
  (H. L. Strack and P. Billerbeck),
  198
Commodus, Emperor, 88
Copper rolls, discovery of at
  Qumran, 182–4
Cullman, O., 199, 223

Damascus, and Qumran, 77
Damascus Document, the, 51, 55,
  58, 76, 77, 122, 123, 125, 131,
  132, 141–5, 147, 204
Dead Sea, 2–3, 69
Dead Sea Scrolls, The Meaning of the
  (A. P. Davies), 31, 192
Dead Sea Scrolls, The (A. Dupont-
  Sommer), 199
de Jonge, M., 205
de Langhe, Prof. R., 27
Demetrius I, 60
Demetrius II, 38, 60, 61
Demetrius III, 60, 61, 169, 191